SOON

SOON

An Overdue History of
Procrastination, from Leonardo
and Darwin to You and Me

ANDREW
SANTELLA

DEY ST.
An Imprint of WILLIAM MORROW

DEY ST.

HarperCollins books may be purchased for educational, business, or sales promotional use. For information, please email the Special Markets Department at SPsales@harpercollins.com.

A hardcover edition of this book was published in 2018 by Dey Street, an imprint of William Morrow.

FIRST DEY STREET PAPERBACK EDITION PUBLISHED 2019.

Designed by Suet Yee Chong

Library of Congress Cataloging-in-Publication Data has been applied for.

ISBN 978-0-06-249159-6

19 20 21 22 23   LSC   10 9 8 7 6 5 4 3 2 1

For A-L

Let's shuck an obligation.

—JOHN BERRYMAN,
"DREAM SONG 82: OP. POSTH. NO. 5"

CONTENTS

1

BARNACLES

My father . . . proposed that I should become a clergyman. He was properly vehement against my turning an idle sporting man, which then seemed my probable destination. I asked for some time to consider.

—CHARLES DARWIN, *THE AUTOBIOGRAPHY OF CHARLES DARWIN*

Even a procrastinator has to start somewhere—*if* he's going to start somewhere—so let's start with Darwin.

Charles Darwin spent much of 1837 drawing, jotting, sketching, and scribbling in one of a series of pocket-size leather-bound notebooks he carried around London with him. Each notebook shut with a small metal clasp, like a diary.

He was living then in rented rooms in a house on Great Marlborough Street, not far from the Athenaeum Club, where rising literary and scientific men gathered to murmur great thoughts to one another amid neoclassical statuary. Darwin had just been elected to membership. One of his new clubmates would be Charles Dickens. I had guessed that the two must have met at some point—you know: Dickens, Darwin, both named Charles—but as far as I can tell, there is no record of it. I like to imagine them in conversation, bewailing the government or the food at the club.

Darwin was just twenty-eight then and had recently returned from a nearly five-year circumnavigation of the globe aboard the HMS *Beagle*, a trip that had made him a minor celebrity in scientific circles. Now he had a book contract and a growing reputation as a naturalist. As a bright and eligible bachelor, he was also getting more dinner invitations than he could accept. And he was still busy trying to make sense of what he had seen on his long voyage. Here's one mystery Darwin spent a lot of time puzzling out: On islands of the Galápagos archipelago, six hundred miles off the west coast of Ecuador, Darwin had found dozens of species of mockingbirds—one species for each island. Why so many varieties in one neighborhood, sharp-beaked birds in one place, blunt-beaked in another? And why had other naturalists found similar variations of iguanas and tortoises and other species, each island's populations different from the next?

These were just the kinds of questions Darwin had been jotting in his leather-bound notebooks, along with drawings and shorthand notes to himself and summaries of conversations with other naturalists. Now he was starting to sketch out some answers, too.

"Each species changes," he wrote in one of his notebooks in the summer of 1838. Three words. Such a simple sentence, but a stunning one, too. Darwin had become convinced that the categories of creatures we know are not immutably fixed articulations of a divine plan, but the result of on-going modification. By September, he had described in his notebooks the mechanism behind that change—the way an organism's environment favors certain random mutations and extinguishes others. He called this culling process natural selection.

This was world-changing, belief-shattering stuff. But twenty years would pass before the world would hear about it. Because Darwin, having made one of the great leaps of intellectual history, did something strange. He dropped the matter. He took no steps to publish his ideas. He sent no treatises to the scientific journals, wrote no essays for the popular press, didn't start writing a book or even seek out a publisher. Not yet, anyway. He did tell a few friends what he was thinking, and he did write a brief summary of his new theory, which he called "a considerable step in science." But he kept this locked away, alongside his metal-clasped notebooks. With it, he placed instructions that his work be published only after his death.

It wasn't like Darwin was idle during this time. He married and started a family. He moved to a house in the country. He stayed back-achingly busy at his writing: He produced volumes on coral reefs and volcanic islands, and a five-part work called *The Zoology of the Voyage of H.M.S. Beagle*. For a periodical called *The Gardeners' Chronicle*, he wrote on some decidedly *not* world-changing topics: how to grow fruit trees from seedlings, for example, and the advantages of using wire rope for well buckets. And from 1846 to 1854, Darwin was almost obsessively engaged in dissecting and describing barnacles.

Darwin devoted whole years to barnacles. He became a barnacle enthusiast. Some might say he teetered on the brink of barnacle obsession. He hunched over a custom-made barnacle microscope all day, surrounded by specimens of barnacles pickled in alcohol, trying to understand the immense variety and mystery of barnacle-dom. He referred to them as "my beloved barnacles." One of his friends said that Darwin had "barnacles on the brain." Darwin spent so long studying barnacles that his children grew up thinking that all fathers lived like this. On a visit to a friend's home, one of Darwin's young kids is supposed to have asked, "But where does your father do his barnacles?"

The barnacles and other matters kept Darwin so busy that it wasn't until 1859 that he finally published *The Origin of Species*, the immensely consequential book that articulated the theory he had first sketched out in his notebooks more than twenty years earlier. Later, when he was old and eminent, Darwin himself confessed that he was puzzled by the delay between the formulation of his ideas and their publication in book form. Some have called this interval the long wait.

So why did Darwin wait so long to let the world know what he had figured out? Why did he put off sharing what he knew to be a monumentally significant scientific advance?

This is a question that preoccupies biographers, historians of science, and anyone interested in the odd ways otherwise rational people—even, as in Darwin's case, fantastically brilliant and prolific ones—behave. A lot of explanations have been offered for Darwin's delay. To begin, there was the very momentousness of his work. Darwin knew as well as anyone that his book would have a revolutionary impact on science and suspected that it would upend the quiet life he had made for himself in the country. It would be easy to understand ambivalence about such a prospect.

Darwin was also the product of a pious Christianity and, though he moved away from faith, he remained the husband of a believer (who worried about her husband's eternal soul) and the loyal son of a devout father. Darwin worried about upsetting the old man. Removing the hand of God from the process of species creation, as his book clearly did, would not have been a step to be taken lightly.

Then there was his perfectionism. Darwin, like any good scientist, was methodical and thorough—see the rows of cabinets full of barnacles to be examined. In Darwin's orderly mind, his decades-long delay would have seemed justified as the due diligence of a scientist who wanted to be sure he got the most important work of his life right. So there was always one more experiment to run, one more re-source to check. And even when he did publish, he insisted on calling his epochal book "an abstract," as if to apologize in advance should anyone find it incomplete.

Or is it that Darwin at first just didn't want to be bothered with publishing? In the parlor at Down House, his home fifteen miles outside London, there was a piano, and in the long hallway, cupboards to hold tennis rackets and hiking boots and notebooks and all the equipment to make British country life livable. There was a billiards room; there were gardens. "My life goes on like clockwork and I am fixed on the spot where I shall end it," he wrote to a friend, sounding like a man completely uninterested in upending his daily routine, let alone all of intellectual history. Clockwork was right. Every day started with a walk out into the country-side before first light; every lunch was preceded by a walk around the gardens with the family dog. In between, and maybe most important, there was work, the little researches he loved. There were barnacles.

In fact, what you see when you begin to look into Darwin's delay is just how busy he kept himself during the time when he was not publishing *The Origin of Species*. Darwin could never really be still, not even in his quiet country retreat, not even when he was putting off his hugely consequential work. Idleness seems to have been hateful to him. What was needed was a project, any project. Earthworms, barnacles, orchids, whatever. He kept at these projects like the world depended on it—even though most of the world couldn't have cared less about Darwin's barnacles. Even Darwin later admitted that he might have overdone it a bit with the barnacles. "I doubt whether the work was worth the consumption of so much time," he conceded in his autobiography. Darwin spent twenty years doing everything but the one thing that he *must* have known really was required of him—publishing his world-changing book about natural selection. In this sense, much of his biography can be read as a story of misspent energies.

So, besides being a prolific scientist, was Darwin also a procrastinator? To answer that question, it helps to understand that procrastination has little to do with laziness.

Not everyone gets this distinction. Bill Wilson, the man who founded Alcoholics Anonymous, once called procrastination "sloth in five syllables." Wilson was right only about the word being a bit of a mouthful. Compounded from two Latin roots (*pro,* meaning "forward," and *cras,* meaning "tomorrow") it takes its time getting to the point, appropriately enough. But Wilson was wrong about the sloth. Procrastinators can keep admirably busy even while they're avoiding their work. Darwin may have been strangely reticent about his new theory, but he can't be called slothful. Again, for evidence, consider the barnacles. The humorist Robert Benchley came closer to the truth in his essay, "How to Get Things Done," which articulates one of the most basic rules of procrastination: "Anyone can do any amount of work, provided it isn't the work he is supposed to be doing at that moment."

Benchley's rule applies to all of us, not just epochally influential scientists.

My apartment is always cleanest, my files most precisely reordered, the fridge most thoroughly cleared of moldering leftovers, when I am under the most pressing deadlines at work. When it is most crucial that I get something done, I become heroically determined to do just about anything *but* that thing.

Darwin is remembered because he was brilliant and diligent and tireless. But it is his delay that makes him so accessible to us, so human. He reminds us of the knottiness of human motivations. We all have our lists of things we should do, things we *must* do. And yet we find some reason to not do them. In this way, we can all claim some kinship with Darwin.

We all have our barnacles.

⸿⸿⸿⸿⸿⸿⸿⸿⸿⸿⸿⸿⸿⸿⸿⸿⸿⸿⸿⸿⸿⸿⸿⸿

I don't recall exactly when it occurred to me to write a book about procrastination, but I do know that for a long time after I had the idea, I did nothing about it.

I made the mistake a lot of procrastinators make: I told friends about my idea. They encouraged me; they told me they couldn't wait to read the book. This was the worst possible thing they could have said. They meant well, but what they didn't understand was that their encouragement only made it *less* likely that I would ever get around to actually writing the book. It wasn't that I doubted it was worth writing. Just the opposite: the more enthusiastic I got about the book, the more difficult, the more impossible, the writing became. I'm the kind of procrastinator who puts off longest that which most urgently needs to be done.

So, when I might have been working on my book about procrastination, I was instead alphabetizing my collection of LPs, or painting a radiator, or watching YouTube videos of someone else's dog barking at a tablespoon. I was vacuuming the stairs or shopping online for Clyde Frazier's basketball shoes. I was sweeping the kitchen floor, unnecessarily. I was eating every last scrap of cheese in our refrigerator, or trying, without success, to repair a dripping faucet. There were even moments when—and this is my deepest, darkest shame—I listened to sports talk radio.

When you go around telling people that you are at work on a book about procrastination, you learn just how common this kind of task avoidance is. People love to confess to procrastination. They can't wait to tell you about their favorite ways to put off what they should be doing. Everyone procrastinates. One bird-watching procrastinator told me that he found an analog for his habit in the natural world: A bird faced with a rival, and unsure whether he should fight or flee, will often do neither. Instead, the bird will peck at the ground. For birds, too, life is a matter of finding something, anything, to do other than the thing you can't bring yourself to do.

In the course of preparing to write (which is to say, *not* write) this book, I mined deep into the literature on the topic—not so much because I am a diligent researcher but because research is everyone's favorite way to put off actual writing. It is a version of pecking at the ground, I suppose. My research turned up the same figures again and again: 20 percent of us are chronic procrastinators; a third of all American undergraduates call themselves severe procrastinators; a hundred minutes of every workday are dithered away by workers. I also noticed that many of the researchers writing about the topic confess to the habit themselves. One of the recurring tropes of academic writing about procrastination is the self-deprecating aside about the delay in writing up research results.

What surprised me most, though, was how many people had dedicated themselves to studying procrastination. A growing pile of journal articles examines the damage done by procrastinators to the economy, to the public health, to our collective emotional vigor. School counselors and life coaches offer solutions for the chronic postponer. Whole shelves could be filled with popular advice books about beating the habit. Maybe the great paradox of procrastination is that it has spawned such a lively mini-industry, and that it keeps so many people so very busy.

Some of my friends got the wrong idea about my plans for this book. They thought I had in mind an advice book—a few anecdotes about high achievers, a summary of the secrets to their success, supported by the latest social scientific research. Follow this example and you, too, can be happy, fulfilled, professionally stellar.

But I really wasn't interested in convincing anyone to do anything or not do anything. In fact, I wasn't even interested in putting a stop to my *own* procrastinating. My aim wasn't to end my habit but to justify it, to excuse it. I hoped that if I looked through enough history and enough scholarship I would be able to find some pretext or rationale for my habitual delay. I understand that this may not be the healthiest attitude, but it's the one that has always come most naturally to me. Self-help books leave me cold: all that business about dutiful achievement and personal advancement. If I really wanted to advance myself, I would have done so by now. But, of course, I haven't—not yet, anyway. And if I had, I probably wouldn't be so interested in procrastination as a topic.

Whenever I face a particularly difficult writing assignment, the first thing I do is go into my bathroom and scrub at the grout between the tiles. It's not that I require a spotlessly clean bathroom, and it's not that this mindless labor helps me think creative thoughts. It's that as long as I am cleaning the grout, I cannot really be expected to be doing anything about the writing project that is troubling me. A person can do only so much, after all.

This need for distraction, this hunger for self-sabotage, goes way back. The most powerful memory of my childhood is of the Sunday-night dread that followed a weekend of procrastination: homework due Monday morning and not a bit of it done. I know now that the homework doesn't end. It's just that at some point we stop calling it homework and someone starts paying us to do it. The dread doesn't go away, either. At least it hasn't for me.

Procrastination is generally considered indefensible. In history and literature, procrastinators have always been portrayed as weak, wasteful, contemptible. We are always under suspicion. Even committed procrastinators can be deeply uncomfortable with the idea of not doing something, which is probably why our foot-dragging is sometimes called killing time. This is an idiom that turns procrastinators into murderers. The language of crime and transgression comes up a lot when people talk about procrastination. The eighteenth-century poet Edward Young called it "the thief of time." The nineteenth-century essayist Thomas De Quincey, whose *Confessions of an English Opium-Eater* pioneered the addiction memoir as a genre and established him as a pretty unassailable expert on transgression, called procrastination "that most odious of vices." He spoke from experience. De Quincey was the sort of committed procrastinator who, when editors wrote him with offers to publish whatever he produced, would never get around to writing back, even though he was desperate for funds.

Darwin, De Quincey: both prolific writers, both procrastinators. What is it about writing that demands deferral? I like to think that no one can understand the mind of the procrastinator quite like a writer who has risked all—career, success, the inviolable deadline—to wait until the last possible moment to begin work. When Dorothy Parker was asked why she was so late turning in a draft, she explained, "Someone else was using the pencil." It's true that I know other writers who are not procrastinators, who are eager to achieve certain milestones by a certain age, to be considered not just successful, but successful while still prodigiously young. My sympathies, though, are with the procrastinator, the late bloomer, the delayer. This book, then, is the product of a life spent postponing what I was supposed to be doing.

This is the book I have spent my whole life not writing.

Procrastination is one of the oldest stories ever told. Whenever in the course of history there has been a job to be done, you could count on finding someone putting off doing it. Procrastination is a theme that bubbles to the surface again and again in literature, religion, economics, medicine, and military history.

Moses, who repeatedly tried to weasel out of the assignments Yahweh had for him, was certainly a procrastinator. The early Greek poet Hesiod, in *The Works and Days,* a poem from 800 B.C. that doubles as a primer in the agricultural arts, warned, "Do not put your work off till tomorrow and the day after, for a sluggish worker does not fill his barn, nor one who puts off his work." Cicero, in an attack on his rival Mark Antony, warned that procrastination is "hateful," especially in a warrior.

The New Testament is filled with admonitions to hurry up, and not put off the important stuff, like repentance. Even the saints have had trouble complying, though. Augustine of Hippo famously prayed for chastity, "but not yet."

The Christian tradition's antipathy to procrastination is rooted in the desire for eternal life—and the fear that if we put off salvation too long, untimely death will intervene and damn us to unending torment. Steeped as I was in this teaching throughout my Catholic boyhood, I am still plagued by the fear that failing to patch the tear in one of my window screens in a timely fashion might be counted as a mortal sin.

What I like about Augustine's chastity prayer is the way it articulates my own ambivalence. Like all procrastinators, and like Augustine, I am always saying, "Not yet." In Samuel Beckett's *Endgame*, Hamm is asked, "Do you believe in the life to come?" He answers, "Mine was always that."

Even many dedicated procrastinators aren't familiar with the history behind their habit. I don't get this. Digging into procrastination's long tradition can be an endlessly distracting effort, which makes it a useful way to avoid doing whatever it is you should be doing instead. Even better, it allows procrastinators to see themselves as upholders of a storied legacy, and not just as addled time-wasters. Cultivating these sorts of rationalizations is crucial to thriving as a procrastinator.

So what's our problem? Thinkers going back to Aristotle have wondered why individuals fail to do what they know is good for them. Why don't we portion our time out wisely so that we accomplish all we are meant to in a timely fashion? Why don't we order our lives rationally?

One answer is: it depends whom you ask. Different disciplines have different ways of trying to answer these questions. I have talked with psychologists and economists, priests and philosophers. Just about everyone has a unique way of understanding procrastination. I have had procrastination explained to me as a physical, a mental, and a cultural experience. I have heard it described as an expression of our genes, as a moral failing, as a weakness of willpower, as a symptom of anxiety or depression, or as the result of a cognitive system overtaxed by external stimuli.

Procrastination is notoriously difficult to define. Most dictionaries say that it means to delay or postpone some action. But most of us understand that procrastination also involves avoiding action because it is in some way onerous— like when I put off seeing my dentist because I dread the drill, or when a student starts a ten-page school essay at nine o'clock the night before it's due. There are people who thrive on this sort of delay, and remain productive despite their procrastination. Some even want to argue that their delay feeds their productivity or that the deadline rush energizes them. But most psychologists who think about this for a living define procrastination as more than just delay. It is postponement undertaken despite expecting to be worse off for the delay. So if you think you have a good reason to put a task off, you're not really procrastinating.

Procrastinating as much as I have, and thinking about procrastination as much as I have—and really, the thinking and the doing are often the same thing—I have learned to see it everywhere. The taxpayer sweating over Form 1040 late on April 15. The homeowner who has been meaning to paint the back porch for years now. The patient putting off the next doctor's appointment. All different, but all procrastinators.

I belong to a tribe of independent workers—writers, editors, coders, graphic designers, tens of millions of us in the United States alone—each of us more or less free to do what we want with our time. So what do we choose to do? Just about anything but what we are supposed to be doing. Maybe we'll go to an afternoon movie or sit around nursing an overpriced Americano. If we have to, we'll even work out. Anything to put off a little longer the inevitability of having to make a living. This gig-economy temporizing comes with a price. Like many procrastinators, I am always alert to the things I haven't gotten around to doing—the books not written, the Internet start-ups not started up. I'm always doing a kind of existential calculation, weighing what I do against what I might have done, or against what I have not yet done.

One reason procrastination is so reviled is that it can lead people off the path proscribed by whoever is in charge. The habit challenges authority, flouts the mandated way of doing things. It is no wonder procrastinators have always attracted powerful enemies. Churches spent a couple thousand years reminding everyone that delay would imperil the soul. Now, obsessed as we are with productivity, we worry about an even more terrible prospect: financial and social loserdom. Psychologists and life coaches and writers of advice books enforce behavioral norms and performance standards that only managers and HR departments could love. In this way, the enterprising efficiency prized in the workplace becomes the foundation of all self-improvement. Productivity is the operative gospel; to be a fully successful human, it is necessary to get things done.

If I had to make a list of things that I find admirable about procrastination, I would begin with this: I like that it seems to bother so many people. I'm for it because so many people are against it. In his 1932 essay, "In Praise of Idleness," Bertrand Russell railed against "the cult of efficiency." I, too, want to applaud procrastinators for their mutiny against the rule of clocks, and for their nonconformity amid all the methodical drones.

But then, I *would* say so, wouldn't I? That is what procrastinators do—attempt to justify their delay with elaborate rationalizations. Procrastinate long enough and you get pretty skilled at this sort of excuse-making. Our talent for self-deception makes procrastination difficult to study, difficult to diagnose, difficult even to define. But thinking deeply about procrastination is worthwhile—and not just as a strategy to postpone real work. It is impossible to think about procrastination for very long without bumping into some fundamental questions: Are we ethically required to make the most of the time allotted to us? How do we reconcile our individual autonomy with our obligations to others and to the relentless demands of a never-ending workday? And, when seemingly all information and every entertainment is available, how do we distinguish between what is worthy of our attention and what is unworthy?

You don't have to be a procrastinator to answer these questions. But it pays to stay alert to deferral's tug, its psychic utility. Like any other compulsion, it lets me feel a simulacrum of control, for a while anyway, when I would otherwise be awash with anxiety. Never mind that the compulsion that helps us feel that sense of control might itself be contributing to the daily chaos that has us so frazzled. You have to reconcile yourself to some paradoxes if you are going to procrastinate. I love procrastinating and hate it; I feel guilty for doing it but am not all that eager to stop.

‖‖‖‖‖‖‖‖‖‖‖‖‖‖‖‖‖‖‖

Procrastinators want heroes. There is nothing I like better than hearing about another procrastinator's shameful time-wasting. If that time-waster happens to be famous and accomplished, even better. To learn about a procrastinator who made it through the dark wood of evasion and delay and made it out the other end and still managed to achieve something: This is the really good stuff. These are the stories that allow the procrastinator to say, "See, it worked for them!" I have become a collector of these stories. They let me understand procrastination not just as a waste of time or as an affront to the prevailing social order or as a way to frustrate oneself (though it can be all those things), but also as a basic human impulse rooted in our native ambivalence and anxiety, and as a tool for navigating the everyday world of obligation. These stories confirm what you, too, may have suspected all along: that even the most wildly productive among us sometimes also manage to be procrastinators.

And why not? An unwavering, dronelike diligence may be great for bees, but not so much for people. There are so many reasons to put off doing something that I sometimes think that the universe must actively want me to procrastinate. Over the twenty minutes it takes me to run a midday errand, my various devices take turns pinging, chiming, buzzing in my pockets and my bags. I could check my phone, my tablet, my watch to see if there is some urgent message to be read— but that would just distract me from my errand, which is itself a distraction from the work I'm supposed to be doing. And who's to say that my work isn't a distraction from something vastly more important? Who's to say that the daily scramble up the greased ramp of achievement isn't itself a pitiable delusion, on scales both personal and societal? I like to think that it is—especially on days when I don't want to work.

When I get home from my errand, I have the option to take a longer walk, a virtual one, up and down the South Island of New Zealand, let's say, via satellite on Google Maps. Every hundred miles or so, when I need a rest, I'll stop and zoom in on whatever pub or café I can find, then cruise around the premises from my satellite's perch. It's amazing how far you can go in an afternoon, and how quickly an afternoon can disappear.

Darwin didn't have access to geospatial digital visualization, but I wonder about his daily walks all the same. He had laid out a sand and gravel path, one-fifth of a mile around his garden in Kent, lined by privet and hazel and holly, and he walked it every day, usually with a fox terrier or two. That was where he went to do his heavy thinking. But I wonder how much thinking he really got done there, what with the dogs underfoot and the kids running around, and the scenic views across meadows and rolling countryside. His kids liked to play cowboys and Indians in the woods along the path and to prank their father by stealing the stones he stacked to count each lap of his walking circuit. God knows how many extra hours Darwin spent circling the garden, like a plane waiting for clearance to land at Heathrow, because of his kids' mischief. It's probably a miracle he published at all.

Darwin loved Down House for what he called its "extreme quietness and rusticity." There he could indulge his lifelong fondness for walking in the woods, but thanks to the growing British rail system and the Penny Post, he could also maintain a professional presence in London. Sometimes the connection remained *too* close for Darwin. His attitude toward the daily tsunami of correspondence the post brought him will be familiar to any present-day beleaguered e-mailer: he depended on it utterly and therefore resented it deeply. When the post one day failed to provide any letters to answer, he told his diary how grateful he was to be left alone for once.

Walking alone in some bosky dell had always been

Darwin's way of putting off the world and its demands on him. As a young man, pressed by his father to choose the ministry or medical school or some other proper career course, Darwin chose none of the above. Instead, he asked for a deferral. He told his father he needed "some time to consider," then went on devoting himself to all the usual country sports of the English gentry—the triumvirate of hobbies his father derided as "shooting, dogs, and rat-catching." At Cambridge, Darwin fell in with a "sporting set" devoted to hunting, riding, drinking, and "singing jolly songs." No professional ambitions seemed to him worth missing the first day of partridge season.

Dithering about life's big decisions has never earned anyone the world's affections. Darwin's father warned him that he might become a disgrace to the family. I have to wonder how much of Darwin's foot-dragging can be read as plain contrariness, a stubborn determination to not give in to the world's mandates. If procrastination has any virtues, one is certainly that it encourages us to think about why we are doing what we are doing (or not doing what we are not). When I put off the things I'm supposed to do, it is often because I'm wondering whether the things the world wants me to do are worth doing at all. Darwin might have been wondering something similar.

It wasn't until he was invited to join the *Beagle* as a "scientific person" and companion to the captain that Darwin found the work that mattered to him. Later in life, after he had become a Great Man, Darwin wondered about the time he had spent putting off the various lives planned for him. He got to thinking about all the time he'd spent among the sporting toffs at Cambridge. "I know that I ought to feel ashamed of days and evenings thus spent," he admitted. But, in fact, Darwin wasn't ashamed. He had decided that he was, on the whole, okay with all the time consumed wondering what to do. He was okay with all the days devoted to jolly song with the sporting set.

Having had so long to think about it, Darwin said he would have done things no differently.

2

||||||||||

MADNESS TO DEFER

Be wise today, 'tis madness to defer
Next day the fatal precedent will plead;
Thus on, till wisdom is pushed out of life:
Procrastination is the thief of time.
—EDWARD YOUNG, *THE COMPLAINT: OR, NIGHT-*
THOUGHTS ON LIFE, DEATH, & IMMORTALITY

Psychology's war on procrastination began in the summer of 1933, or so one could argue, when a lonely nineteen-year-old named Albert Ellis kept trying to start conversations with women in the New York Botanical Garden.

Ellis is now remembered as one of the twentieth century's most influential psychologists. But in 1933, he was just an anonymous business student with a debilitating fear of speaking to women. At the time, Ellis lived with his parents in the Bronx, not far from the garden, and he made a habit of sitting on benches there, wishing he had the nerve to approach any of the women he saw strolling among the roses. Ellis desperately wanted to meet these women, date them, maybe even marry one of them.

"But no matter how much I told myself the time was ripe to approach," Ellis recounted in a paper he presented at a professional conference more than a half century later, "I soon copped out and walked away, cursing myself for my abysmal cowardice."

Distraught, Ellis devised what he called "a homework assignment" for himself. He would go to the botanical garden every day in July, as long as it wasn't raining, and whenever he saw a woman sitting on a park bench, he would sit on the same bench and give himself one minute to initiate a conversation. Ellis would allow himself no excuses, no evasions, no wiggle room.

"I was giving myself no time to procrastinate about trying, no time to ruminate and thereby to build up my worrying," he wrote.

Ellis did it. He talked—or tried to—with 130 women

in the botanical garden that summer. Thirty of them walked away immediately. But Ellis managed to start conversations with 100 of the women he approached. To his amazement, one actually agreed to go on a date with him—though she never showed up. Ellis nevertheless considered his experiment a success. He had learned that he could overcome his anxiety by confronting the very thing—talking to women—that paralyzed him. The experience changed Ellis's life, "and in some ways changed the history of psychotherapy," he later said.

Ellis was born in Pittsburgh in 1913 to an emotionally distant father who was often away on business and a mother he described as "a bustling chatterbox who never listened." Ellis recalled that, to fill the void left by his parents' inattention, he took charge of his two younger siblings, waking early with the help of an alarm clock he bought himself so that he could dress them for the day. Ellis's image of himself was heroic.

He graduated from the City College of New York in 1934 with a bachelor's degree in business, but after some failed efforts to publish fiction, earned a Ph.D. in clinical psychology from Teachers College of Columbia University in 1947. Ellis's career as a psychologist began conventionally enough by the standards of the time. He practiced in a classical psychoanalytic mode—listening to a couch-bound analysand recount dreams, fantasies, and free associations in an effort to access the unconscious roots of irrationality. But Ellis grew frustrated by his inability to produce results for his patients. Maybe more significantly, he seemed constitutionally unsuited to the long slog of therapy. So he began preaching a more dynamic, "highly active approach to problem-solving, rather than waiting for a miracle," as he and co-author William Knaus wrote in the introduction to their 1977 book, *Overcoming Procrastination*. The approach Ellis used to cure himself of his fear of talking to women became a foundation of what he called rational emotive behavior therapy, a way of addressing the irrational beliefs that produce self-defeating behavior.

By the late 1950s, he was teaching his new methods to other therapists. Ellis's timing was good; the world would soon be ready for an alternative to Freud. Psychoanalysis would become so suspect in the next several decades that the Nobel Prize–winning zoologist Peter Medawar spoke for many when he called it "the most stupendous intellectual confidence trick of the 20th century."

Ellis, always blunt, liked to say that "Freud was full of shit." He had little use for years spent talking on a couch. Ellis's prescription: "forgetting your god-awful past" and taking action. Neurosis, he said, was "a high-class word for whining." People who wanted to plumb their childhood traumas were "big babies."

As Ellis's influence grew, his acolytes enthusiastically emulated his self-help assignments. For better or worse, some reenacted his botanical garden exercise, launching themselves at unsuspecting women in an attempt at achieving psychological wholeness—and maybe also getting a date. Pickup methodology aside, Ellis's most enduring contribution may have been to inject a sense of urgency and action to the practice of psychology. Just as, at nineteen, he cured his shyness by giving himself "no time to ruminate and thereby to build up my worrying," so throughout his career he cultivated an image as a robust, no-nonsense dynamo who prescribed action over talk, effort over contemplation.

Ellis's approach was one of the progenitors of cognitive behavioral therapy (CBT), the predominant mode of psychological treatment practiced today. If at any time in the last couple decades you have sought help with insomnia, depression, anxiety, substance abuse, the inability to sustain relationships—whatever—you have likely taken a turn through the CBT workout. CBT aims to identify and eliminate the unproductive habits of thought that produce unhealthy behavior and self-destructive moods. It's not hard to understand why the cognitive therapies pioneered by Ellis and others (such as Aaron Beck) became so popular. They offered a quicker, cheaper, less cerebral alternative to traditional psychotherapy, with its high fees, arcane methodologies, and seemingly endless rounds of talk. Where the old way demanded years of conversation about your childhood, your dreams, and your unspoken desires, the new therapies promised results with a course of workbook exercises and some highly structured meetings with a therapist.

Practitioners of CBT like to describe it as "solution-oriented," and there is indeed something briskly businesslike about all the lists, inventories, self-tests, and survey questions you find in a CBT workbook. It is a kind of therapy almost guaranteed to appeal to MBAs. It's efficient.

Dig into the literature on procrastination and you'll find references to a book by Paul Ringenbach called *Procrastination Through the Ages: A Definitive History*. You'll have trouble finding the book itself, though. It never existed. Ringenbach's bogus title was a publishing-industry inside joke, a hoax: no dawdling writer would ever get around to finishing a definitive history of procrastination.

Nevertheless, in *Overcoming Procrastination*, Ellis and

Knaus dismiss Ringenbach's nonexistent book, as if they had considered it carefully: It is "an interesting survey, but it sheds little light on coping with the problem," they write. Faulty bibliography aside, Ellis and Knaus were right to claim that there had been a dearth of books on "coping with the problem" before *Overcoming Procrastination*. But *Overcoming* would be the first of many volumes to follow that would declare war on the habit and offer strategies to defeat it. Despite its continuing influence, *Overcoming* has not aged well. It is peppered with jargon that deserves to be cataloged in a treasury of seventies-era pop psychology clichés. I'm not sure what the authors meant by "self-downing," for example, but the phrase does evoke a certain time. And the authors have an odd and dispiriting habit of spelling out words to show emphasis: "you'd better spell life h-a-s-s-l-e" and "the process of change involves considerable work in developing more of a long-range hedonistic outlook. Yes, w-o-r-k!"

In *Overcoming*, Ellis proposes homework assignments not unlike the one he gave himself to beat his fear of speaking to women: penalize yourself for procrastinating by promising to do something you don't like to do (one example from the book suggests you send a $50 donation to the Klan every time you put off what you should be doing) or develop a system of rewards for not procrastinating as a way of conditioning yourself to "automatically" do the tasks you have been putting off. These strategies, and others like them, show up regularly in the psychological and economic literature of procrastination that would emerge in the following decades.

Overcoming and its progeny tackle procrastination systematically, like a logistics problem. There is something beguiling, even irresistible, about such a methodical program. Who hasn't dreamed the dream of self-actualization? Who hasn't vowed to get serious, buckle down, set some goals, do some sit-ups? Most of us have accumulated and discarded our own small libraries of self-improvement. The urge is as natural as the need to procrastinate, its twin. But my problem has always been with the system itself, as manifested in CBT workbook exercises, self-tests, personal inventories, and statements of objectives. Take the workbooks, for starters: What adult wants to complete a *workbook,* suggesting as they do all the indignities of fourth-grade phonics? Workbooks are things to be used by preadolescents, names penciled at the top of the perforated-edge page in a graceless Palmer Method scribble. You hunch over your workbook in your molded one-piece desk-chair combo with the clamshell top that can be raised to briefly shield you from the teacher's monitoring eye. But beyond a certain age—let us say, twelve?—one should no longer be required to complete workbooks.

More to the point, the problem with too many systems of self-improvement is that they have no use for so much of the stuff that makes life such a precious mess: the ambiguities, the ruminating, the unrealized desires. For Ellis, procrastination was a failing, a deviation from a desired norm. For someone as invested in his own heroic self-conception, procrastination was intolerable. It was "abysmal cowardice." The cognitive-behavioral playbook he helped develop attacks unwanted behaviors by challenging the beliefs and patterns of thought that produce them. The panicked flyer, the fear-frozen public speaker, the recalcitrant ditherer is asked: What evidence do you have to support your way of thinking? Might there be another way of thinking that would be more healthy? It's all common sense. But as any procrastinator or panicked flyer will tell you, those patterns of thought are usually buried pretty deep, in a place where common sense doesn't easily penetrate.

In retrospect, I can see that going to talk to Joe Ferrari about my love affair with procrastination was from the beginning fraught with difficulty, like scheduling an appointment with the family physician to discuss your plan to smoke an additional two packs a day.

Ferrari is a professor at DePaul University in Chicago and might be the world's most prolific writer and researcher on procrastination. Look in any bibliography on the topic and you'll see his name over and over: Ferrari, J.

Ferrari was one of the first people I called after I decided to write about procrastination. I had read an advice book he'd published, suggesting ways procrastinators could overcome their habit. I figured Ferrari could tell me how his discipline had become so invested in procrastination. He agreed to meet me on one of his visits to New York, and I told him I would pick him up at LaGuardia in my well-worn Corolla and drive him wherever he wanted to go. When I met him at the airport, he was carrying, under one arm, a copy of Max Engammare's *On Time, Punctuality, and Discipline in Early Modern Calvinism*, which he presented to me. Accepting his gift, I wondered if Ferrari had noticed I had been a couple minutes late to Arrivals.

Our plan was to drive to a diner in Woodside, a tidy neighborhood wedged between two cemeteries and the Brooklyn-Queens Expressway. Even though he was the out-of-towner, Joe seemed more certain about the best route to take, so I followed his directions: where to turn, when to change lanes, how much farther. And when he wasn't guiding me through Queens, he was sharing his store of knowledge about procrastinators.

"I call them procs," he told me between directions. "They are often very smart people. They have to be, to keep coming up with their plausible excuses."

Ferrari has been writing and talking and teaching about procrastination so frequently and for so long that he has developed an understandably proprietary view of the field. I came to like Joe and admire his enthusiasm for his topic, but I sometimes had the feeling during that first meeting that he took anyone's procrastination, especially mine, as a personal affront.

Ferrari became interested in procrastination while he was a graduate student in psychology at Adelphi University in New York in the 1980s. During a classroom discussion of self-defeating behaviors, he asked one of his professors if anyone had ever studied procrastination as a self-handicapping strategy. The professor directed Ferrari to the library to find out for himself. What Ferrari found surprised him.

"There was nothing," Joe told me. "What little I found was about writer's block, that sort of thing." Figuring he could have the field largely to himself, Ferrari made procrastination and self-handicapping his area of study. Self-handicapping, he explained to me, refers to the ways people defeat themselves—maybe because they are afraid to fail or because they are afraid to succeed at whatever task is at hand. Self-handicapping procrastinators might postpone work on projects that they believe are beyond their capabilities. It's not just fear of the projects that paralyzes them. It's that their procrastination protects them from failure. Should they fail, it will be because they didn't really try, because they waited until the last minute, because they said, "Screw this." Their procrastination excuses their failure, even as it contributes to it.

"This is one way people protect themselves from their anxieties," Ferrari told me. "The chronic procrastinator would rather have other people think he lacks effort than that he lacks ability."

Procs turned out to be worthy subjects for research. But when Ferrari began presenting his first papers on the topic at academic conferences, he was disappointed to find that procrastination wasn't always taken seriously as a topic of study. He heard the same lame jokes again and again about his chosen subject. At one conference, an organizer told Ferrari that his presentation would have to wait until the very end, "because, you know, it's on procrastination." Even today, Ferrari is reluctant to tell someone he has just met—say the person in the neighboring seat on a cross-country flight—that he researches procrastination. He doesn't want to hear the one-liners, the riddles. ("Heard the one about the procrastinator? I'll tell you later . . .") He told me about hearing some ersatz life coach on the radio joking about procrastination and its discontents. Joe was not amused.

"It's not funny and it's not helpful," he said. "You should see the e-mails I get. People are suffering because of this habit. It causes real harm."

Ferrari has worked for more than a quarter century to help make procrastination studies a respected and respectable research field. He has seen it mature as an academic subdiscipline. He was at the head of a new wave of academic researchers who added social-scientific data to the clinical observations of practitioners like Ellis. In 1999 Ferrari attended the first of what would become biannual international meetings of procrastination researchers. At that first meeting, in Germany, 12 academics showed up. The 2015 meeting, also in Germany, attracted 180 procrastination researchers.

The field has grown to include not just psychologists, but neuroscientists, geneticists, and behavioral economists. A 2011 study by Laura Rabin of Brooklyn College took a neuropsychological approach to procrastination, finding a correlation between procrastination and failures of executive function, the planning and self-control processes centered in the brain's frontal lobe. Fuschia Sirois of the University of Sheffield has considered procrastination as a risk factor for general health and well-being. A 2014 study by researchers from the University of Colorado found that procrastination and impulsivity are genetically linked, and that the tendency to procrastinate can be passed from one generation to the next. Like any self-respecting academic field, it has spawned feuds and controversies. If you want to start a heated argument among a group of procrastination researchers, ask whether chronic deferral has more to do with our inability to manage time or with a failure to regulate our emotions.

Ferrari comes down on the side of the latter. "Telling a chronic procrastinator to 'just do it' is like telling a depressed person, 'Hey, c'mon, cheer up!'"

To understand procrastination, he says, you have to look not at the procrastinator's environment but inside the procrastinator. When you do, he argues, you see that procrastination is rooted in unmanaged moods and emotions. People delay because they think they have to be in the right mood to get something done. They convince themselves that their mood will change in the future, so the future would be a more suitable time to act. Our delay is rooted in our attempt to manage our moods and to fit them to the tasks we face: If I take a nap now, I'll be able to focus better later. Tweeting now will help me warm up for the writing to follow.

Again and again in his work, Ferrari has explored ways that procrastination can be deployed as a way to deal with our anxieties or protect ourselves from feared outcomes. The problem is that the procrastinator's attempt at self-defense usually turns out to be perversely self-defeating. A study by Ferrari and Diane Tice showed that college students were more likely to put off preparing for a test when they were told that it was a meaningful evaluation of their abilities than when they were told the same test was meaningless and being taken only for fun. That is, when the test counted, procrastinators procrastinated; when it didn't, they acted like nonprocrastinators. Only when their efforts mattered did the procrastinators bother to subvert their own efforts. The more that was at stake, the more desperately procrastinators needed to protect themselves, paradoxically, by not trying too hard.

I recognized the rationalization from my own life. It made sense to see the habit as rooted in moods, anxiety, or depression. I had scribbled in my notebook a line from an essay by the writer Robert Hanks that had impressed me: "I put things off because much of the time I'm frightened and sad."

Reading Ferrari led me to the work of another academic psychologist, Timothy Pychyl, who has suggested that instead of letting mood dictate behavior, procrastinators would do better to remember that behavior shapes mood. Doing the thing you have been trying to put off doing will make you feel better. In fact, it is about the *only* thing that will make you feel better. The problem, I knew too well, is that it is also probably the one thing you can't imagine doing.

Here's how it would go for me: Having sat down at my desk to write, I would decide that what was really necessary was a new pot of coffee. The coffee-making would require a trip to the kitchen. Once in the kitchen, I couldn't help but notice the burned-out lightbulb over the counter. Replacing the lightbulb would require a trip to the corner shop. No way could I walk to the corner to get a new lightbulb, though; I had writing to do. On the other hand, the store was next to a really outstanding bagel place, and what with the coffee being made, it would be hard to argue with the need for bagels. Also, on the same block as the corner shop and bagel place was the bookstore where I could spend a little time browsing among the anthologies. It might even be inspiring.

Even as I lead myself down this mental cul-de-sac, I am aware of the self-deception that I am practicing. Not that it matters. Work is the one thing that will set me right. Work is also, at times, the one thing I would do anything to avoid.

One of the most influential studies about self-handicapping doesn't have to do with procrastination at all. In a 1978 paper called "Control of Attributions About the Self Through Self-Handicapping Strategies: The Appeal of Alcohol and Underachievement," Edward Jones and Steven Berglas argued that some misuse of alcohol could be understood as an attempt to save face by exploiting drinking as an excuse for failure. "By finding or creating impediments that make good performance less likely, the strategist nicely protects his (or her) sense of self-competence," they wrote.

Berglas understood the impulse from personal experience, he said; he himself first experimented with drugs in high school just before taking the SAT, a test on which he was expected to get a perfect score. The drug-taking became an excuse, a way to lower the freighted expectations without compromising his sense of himself as intelligent. His pre-SAT high provided the seed for the theory.

Procrastinators employ the same strategy: we protect our sense of our own competence by making it very, very hard for ourselves to succeed. It's just one example of the twisted logic of procrastination. You have to marvel at all the many reasons you can find to procrastinate.

Maybe I do because I am a perfectionist afraid of falling short of my own high expectations for myself.

Or I am an excuse-maker who delays so as to give myself an explanation for the failure I am sure will come.

Or I have a very public task to perform and I procrastinate because I fear the evaluation of others.

Or I resent having to answer to my boss or my spouse or the credit card company or some other authority that expects something of me by a certain date.

Or I get off on the adrenaline rush that comes with trying to do things at the last moment.

Or I am overwhelmed by the size and number of jobs to be done.

Or I simply find doing what I am supposed to do a huge pain in the ass.

And to make things more complicated, I could be the most conscientious person in the world about, say, meeting my professional obligations, but a perennial laggard about household tasks. One of my pet theories—or to put it another way, one of my self-justifying rationalizations—is that procrastination can feel like a necessary ritual, a passage to be endured on the way to accomplishment. Like any ritual, it appeals to us as a way of controlling, in some small way, a life that can feel chaotic and unmanageable.

In fact, what I noticed was that just about all the explanations I encountered made some kind of sense to me. A psychologist named Piers Steel staked out a position that emphasized our collective predilection for the present, not our inability to regulate mood, as key to procrastination. "It is largely because we view the present in concrete terms and the future abstractly that we procrastinate" was the sentence that I had underlined in his book. This too made a certain sense to me. Just about *all* of the theories made some sense. Even the theories that directly contradicted other sensible theories still somehow made sense to me. To read the literature is to recognize myself in so many, many diagnoses.

And still I kept putting things off.

One morning not long ago, I reached, half-awake, for my laptop, as I usually do. Waiting for me online was some algorithm's idea of a joke: a link to an article explicating the eight habits of highly productive people. I closed the clamshell and I went back to my pillow, face-first. I never did read the article, but I would bet that rolling over and going back to sleep was not one of the recommended habits.

I don't have to jump at every bit of clickbait I encounter to know how completely the language of business management now defines self-improvement. The ideal promoted in airport bookstalls and viral videos involves a more productive, more punctual me. It stigmatizes any variation toward the individual and idiosyncratic.

I remember trying to explain to Ferrari why the merging

of popular self-improvement with managerial imperatives left me skeptical. Wouldn't anyone who aspired to independent thought feel obliged to resist the constant exhorting to be faster, better, and a more model drone?

"Yeah, that's what we call being reactant," Ferrari told me. "That's when you say, 'If you tell me to do this, well then, I'm gonna do just the opposite.'"

"But some of the most fun I've had in my life has been doing the things I wasn't supposed to be doing," I countered. Ferrari looked a little alarmed, but I went on. "I just mean making my own choices. Don't you think that deferring or declining or postponing can be an active choice, a way of constructing yourself?"

No, he didn't think so.

"Look, there are real costs to procrastination," Ferrari said. "There are economic costs, yes, but the personal costs are huge. In relationships. In self-worth. Life is short. Have you made a difference in the world?"

I wasn't prepared to stake my argument on the thin evidence of my personal contributions to the universal good. So I said nothing. But later I thought of something that every procrastinator knows: sometimes the best things you do are the things you do only to put off doing something else.

I'm not sure how social-science researchers would quantify a paradox like that. I want to understand myself as an individual, not as science and social science would understand me, as an example of a general type. My procrastination is to me subtle and subjective and mysterious and unknowable. But then, I would think so. I am a procrastinator, which means I know how to rationalize my habit.

Jones and Berglas seemed to be getting at something like this point when they wrote that all of us have a "need for certain kinds of ambiguity to allow room for self-sustaining and self-embellishing fantasies."

Freud recognized that patients wanted it both ways: having come to the doctor seeking help, they would do their best to keep the doctor from helping them at all. Procrastination has always been a favorite tactic for analysands hoping to obstruct their own analysis. Knowing you have fifty minutes of the doctor's time, you spend almost all of it talking about inconsequential stuff. Only at the very last minute, if at all, do you bring up what you really want to discuss. When you consider the vulnerability of the analysand's position—lying down maybe, being operated on in a sense—stall tactics are understandable. *Hold on. I'm not quite ready for this.*

But the analyst can delay, too. The French psychoanalyst Jacques Lacan, wanting to control the pace of treatment, introduced his notorious "short sessions," in which the analyst abruptly interrupts the unsuspecting patient and dismisses her. How short were Lacan's short sessions? That was up to Lacan. In his book, *Jacques Lacan: The Death of an Intellectual Hero,* Stuart Schneiderman, a former analysand, recounted how Lacan ended one session by rising from his chair and announcing that the two were finished for the day. Schneiderman had just begun talking.

The end of a Lacanian session had meaning, at least for Lacan. He wanted his analysands to wonder: *What did I say to make my doctor cut me off so soon?* The question would dangle in the interval between sessions, ripening for discussion by the next meeting.

So too would other questions, such as Do I still have to pay for an hour of analysis, if I get only five minutes? For the record, Lacan didn't seem too concerned about the money questions. Schneiderman recalls him sitting at his desk, counting bank notes during sessions.

Preoccupied as I was becoming with procrastination, I wondered if Lacan had located a previously underappreciated power in postponement. Where his analytical colleagues had allowed their fearful, unready analysands to waste their time, Lacan adopted delay as a therapeutic strategy. By abruptly ending the session, in effect postponing the session, he had made the session more potent.

I took that as further evidence of a truth I had begun to recognize: no matter how much you deplore procrastination in others, you can always find a good reason to do it yourself.

SAINTS, CROWS, POETS, PRIESTS

We will labor now. Alas, it is too late.

—EDGAR ALLAN POE, "THE IMP OF THE PERVERSE"

On a road in fourth-century Armenia, the story goes, a Roman centurion met a talking crow. The officer had resolved to convert to Christianity, but now this eloquent crow had come to urge him not to do anything rash. The crow had an idea for the centurion: Delay the conversion; don't rush. Maybe take a day to think about it.

The centurion, though, would not be put off. He insisted on starting his new life as a believer immediately.

Realizing that the crow was, in fact, the Devil in avian form arrived to tempt him, the centurion—who would later be venerated as St. Expedite, patron saint of procrastinators—did something remarkable. He stomped the talking bird to death.

I learned about St. Expedite early in my research. I was raised Catholic and educated in Catholic schools and had read countless lives of countless saints, but I had no idea there was a patron saint of procrastinators. It made a kind of sense, though. Any guilt-plagued procrastinator knows what it is to worry about the cost of delay. Will I miss the deadline that I ignored too long? Will I fail the exam for which I prepared too late? In St. Expedite's story the stakes were raised, the price of procrastination inflated. For Expedite, delay meant risking his very soul. The story of St. Expedite and the talking crow made procrastination a matter of spiritual life and death.

The more I thought about the saint and his talking crow, the more I appreciated the mythic gravitas his legend brought to my commonplace habit. Expedite made me feel ennobled. Procrastination as understood in the context of St. Expedite stood in for the most basic conflicts between the temporal and the eternal, the rapacious body and the imperiled soul. This seemed like a promising thread for the self-justifying procrastinator to pursue.

I soon found out that the Saint Who Refused to Delay is the object of a devotional cult that spans several continents. On tiny Réunion Island in the Indian Ocean, believers build roadside altars in Expedite's honor, always painted bright red and decorated with small statues of the saint. They are part of an elaborate protocol of intercessory prayer and bargaining. The way it works is this: You pay homage to the saint by constructing a roadside altar complete with a figurine of Expedite, then ask for his help in getting what you want. If, despite your homage to Expedite, your prayers go unanswered, the local tradition is to decapitate the figurine. This explains why headless statues of St. Expedite are so easy to find on Réunion Island.

In São Paulo, Brazil, the system is slightly different. Worshippers crowd services on St. Expedite's feast day to leave scribbled prayers at church altars imploring the saint's help. (The Feast of St. Expedite is celebrated on April 19, just a few days after another key date for American procrastinators—tax-filing day in the United States.)

The locus of devotion to St. Expedite in the United States is in Louisiana, where his cult draws on a syncretic mingling of Catholic and voodoo influences. Nowhere does it thrive more fully than in New Orleans. The irony of this is too obvious to make a big deal about: somehow you have to go to America's capital of revelry and good times rolling to understand how punctuality can be the basis of a kind of faith.

In New Orleans, it's not hard to find prayer cards printed with ready-made invocations to the erstwhile centurion:

> Saint Expedite,
> Noble Roman youth, martyr,
> You who quickly bring things to pass,
> You who never delays, I come to you in need . . .

Or

> St. Expedite, witness of Faith to the point of
>   martyrdom, in exercise of Good, you make
>   tomorrow today.
> You live in the fast time of the last minute, always
>   projecting yourself toward the future.
> Expedite and give strength to the heart of the
>   man who doesn't look back and who doesn't
>   postpone.

The most impressive thing about St. Expedite may be that he inspires all this devotion having never, most likely, really existed. Catholic authorities concede that St. Expedite is an assemblage of myths and legends, with little basis in fact. Nevertheless, the early church deployed St. Expedite as the focus of a kind of fourth-century marketing campaign to broadcast its antiprocrastination creed. His image was supposed to persuade pagans of the need not to put off their salvation, to convert promptly, before it became too late.

Today, one of the best-known statues of St. Expedite lives in a small church on the scruffy edge of New Orleans's French Quarter, where the scent of spilled beer hangs heavy on the streets. Our Lady of Guadalupe Church is the city's oldest, built in 1826 as a funeral chapel. Its statue of St. Expedite occupies a small niche in the back of the church, and when I flew to New Orleans to visit the saint, I found about a dozen intercessory prayers written on bits of paper and left at the base of the statue. They had been dropped there by visitors who had come to the church to ask for Expedite's help in some urgent matter or other—beating their drinking habit or escaping some legal difficulty or, of course, overcoming their tendency to procrastinate.

I had been told that it was local custom for the devout to leave a pound cake by the statue as an offering to the saint. But that day I found no pound cake among the scribbled prayers. There in the spooky old church, surrounded by flickering candles, I briefly wondered if all the proffered cakes had been accepted and consumed by St. Expedite through some miracle.

It turns out that there is a less supernatural explanation. The job of removing pound cake and other offerings from the foot of the statue belongs to Father Anthony Rigoli, the church's pastor, known locally as Father Tony. Cleaning up after petitioners appears nowhere on Father Tony's official job description, but I guess one does what has to be done. He is a member of the Missionary Oblates of Mary Immaculate, an organization of priests dedicated to preaching to the poor. As pastor of Our Lady of Guadalupe, he has inherited by default all the responsibilities that come with managing the best-known St. Expedite shrine in North America.

I had made arrangements to talk with him one afternoon in the week before Mardi Gras. Making the short walk from my hotel to the church, early in the afternoon, I had the chance to watch overserved tourists stagger down the sidewalks, which is a kind of New Orleans spectator sport. The run up to the annual pre-Lenten climax of revelry had begun. The city's immoderation seemed magnified.

In the middle of all this humid partying, the modest church on Rampart Street was a cool refuge. I had arranged to meet Father Tony in the small gift shop next door to the church, where visitors can browse through prayer books, saints' medals, and prayer cards—kind of a Barnes & Noble for the pious. While I was waiting, I picked up a small pewter St. Expedite medal and a devotional card with a ready-made prayer to the saint: "... *that we may, by the intercession of St. Expedite, be conducted with courage, fidelity, and promptitude, at the time proper and favourable and come to a good and happy end, through our Lord, Jesus Christ. Amen.*"

Before he came to Our Lady of Guadalupe fourteen years ago, Father Tony had not heard of St. Expedite. But once at work at the church, he quickly grew accustomed to the tour buses cruising by on Rampart Street, telling their version of the Expedite story: one day in the nineteenth century, a package arrived at the New Orleans church containing a statue of an unknown saint. Since the package bore only the postal instruction "expedite," the mystery saint was soon given that name himself. It is a story for which the pastor has little use.

Neat and gray-haired and energetic, Father Tony was wearing a New Orleans Saints sweatshirt over his clerical collar when he found me wandering the gift shop and introduced himself. Cheering for the Saints (the football team, not the holy people) had been one of Father Tony's concessions to the local culture, and not one he made easily, having grown up a Bills fan in Buffalo. In New Orleans's distinctive brew of cultures and faiths, it helps to maintain a certain flexibility for crossovers and hybridization. Some of St. Expedite's most devoted followers in New Orleans aren't Catholics at all, but practitioners of voodoo. They sometimes come into the gift shop at Our Lady of Guadalupe seeking black candles for their rites.

I asked Father Tony if he believed leaving pound cakes for St. Expedite was an effective strategy for getting what one wanted. He rolled his eyes toward heaven.

"People get confused about these devotions, because they can border on superstitions," he said. He tried to clarify. "I don't think saints answer prayers, but I do think Jesus does. When we ask someone to pray for us, what we're really asking for is support. We all want to feel that support. So these devotions are really for our sake. And that's okay. But I think the Lord has bigger things to worry about."

The Catholic world in which I was raised had little use for tardiness. In my Catholic grade school, brilliance was tolerated, but punctuality revered. Nothing was more important than being on time. Every once in a while you would run across some nun who was so fanatical about punctuality that she insisted all her students be in their homeroom seats five minutes before the school day was to start. This was the sort of hyperpunctuality that turned actual punctuality into tardiness. We thought of it as nun time.

The clock was our enemy in those days. It seemed determined to frustrate us. The classroom clock was almost always positioned, not coincidentally, just below the crucifix that watched over us. In the most tedious classes, when we longed most desperately for release, the minute hands always seemed to stall. When we needed *more* time, say to complete a test or finish an in-class essay, the clock betrayed us by seeming to gain pace. I know you don't have to be a Catholic schoolkid to feel betrayed by the clock; school days can seem interminable anywhere. But enduring as much talk of eternity as we did left us, I think, especially worried that three o'clock might never come.

Father Tony told me that not long before my visit, he had preached about a reading from the Gospel of Mark: the story about Jesus encountering the sibling fishermen Simon and Andrew along the Sea of Galilee. Jesus had invited them to abandon their livelihoods and to join him in his itinerant ministry. The brothers did not delay. "Immediately they left their nets and followed Him," says the Gospel.

"It says *immediately*," Father Tony went on. "They dropped what they were doing *that instant* to follow Jesus. Think about what they were being asked to do. They were supposed to give up their livelihoods, everything they knew. And yet there was no hesitation."

Few of us measure up to such a model of dispatch. Father Tony confessed to me that back when he was teaching high school students, he tended to put off grading his students' papers. I told him that I thought this was the kind of bad habit that could be justified, considering that many of the students had probably themselves waited until the last minute to do their work.

It was at this point that I decided I might as well unburden myself of a secret, to make my own confession to Father Tony. So I came clean: I told Father Tony I had put off having this very conversation. The shameful truth was that I had made an earlier, unproductive reportorial trip to New Orleans—unproductive because of my habitual procrastination.

What had happened was this: When I had first learned about the St. Expedite statue at Our Lady of Guadalupe, I had come down to New Orleans from Brooklyn, with my buddy Mike, a friend since high school. Mike is a writer, too, but unlike me, he's no procrastinator. Mike had inspired my visit to New Orleans. Over dinner one night, he'd told me about his plans for a new book, a book that would require him to travel to Israel to do research. I praised Mike's idea for the book, encouraged him to go to Israel, and figured nothing would come of it. A few days later, Mike e-mailed me from Israel.

I was amazed. He might as well have e-mailed from the moon. There was no circumstance under which I could imagine deciding to go halfway around the world on short notice to pursue some germ of an idea that had just come to me.

I have always envied travelers like Mike, and the ease with which they pick themselves up and get around the world. I envy their e-mails that casually mention, "I'm in Amsterdam." I envy their ability to beg out of a lunch date by saying, "Sorry, I'll be in Bangkok that day." Because I am a procrastinator, travel doesn't come easily to me and it is one of the things I most frequently put off until some future date, a date that often never comes. It would be only fair if travel procrastinators like me could collect some official tag or stamp or ticket, something like those old steamer-trunk stickers, but in our case representing each of the places we have *not* gone. I have not gone to Paris or Rome or Tokyo. Last fall, I didn't go to Princeton, New Jersey.

It was Mike who convinced me that I had to go to New Orleans for my book. And knowing how likely I was to put off such a trip, he insisted on going with me. So it was that a few weeks later, Mike and I found ourselves in Our Lady of Guadalupe Church in New Orleans, staring at the statue of St. Expedite. My vague plan had been to talk to some of the locals—a priest, a parishioner, anyone I spotted leaving a piece of pound cake for St. Expedite—as part of my journey into the history of procrastination.

But once in New Orleans, I found I didn't really want to talk to anybody. I had what seemed like better things to do. Mostly those things involved eating and drinking. An entire city of Sazeracs and po'boys beckoned, and I felt it would be rude not to answer. And so it was that, a day and a half later, and despite Mike's evident mystification, we left New Orleans without having spoken with anyone about St. Expedite.

And this is why I'd had to come to New Orleans a *second* time, this time alone, but having taken the precautionary measure of making an appointment to speak with Father Tony. (As a type, the journalist who is reluctant to talk to his sources offers a deep and heretofore untapped reservoir of farcical comedy and pathos for novelists or screenwriters in search of subjects.)

Father Tony understood. Even the best of us sometimes indulge in this kind of inexplicable foot-dragging. Even when we think we know what we should do, something inside us prevents it. To draw on the early church for an example: St. Augustine's stubborn commitment to thievery, hedonism, and promiscuity. He couldn't help himself. "I loved my own error," Augustine wrote of his wild youth.

Rejecting the wishes of his mother that he marry respectably, Augustine instead undertook a fifteen-year-long affair with a woman who bore him a son. Augustine's mother prayed unceasingly for her son's conversion and when she died, he was racked with guilt for having lived so wantonly and for having put off conversion so long, despite his mother's prayers. The dominant motif of the *Confessions* is Augustine's self-reproach for his hitherto wasted life and for his delay in accepting Christian belief. "Too late have I loved Thee, O Lord," he wrote, in an expression that would echo through centuries of Christian hymns and prayers.

Augustine's anguish is recognizable to anyone who has waited too long to do something important, who has seen a crucial moment pass unseized, let an opportunity pass. It was Augustine who gave us the idea of original sin, a theology that any procrastinator could appreciate, premised as it is on the hard-to-refute assertion that there is something really, essentially wrong with all of us. Augustine, by the way, spent about fifteen years working on a series of studies of the Book of Genesis—roughly the same investment of time Darwin made in his barnacles—and, like Darwin, resisted completing and publishing his work long after his friends told him to wrap it up already and move on.

Augustine's real twin isn't Darwin, but the legendary

Expedite. Augustine and Expedite make a saintly Odd Couple—one who left an indelible mark on Western intellectual history and one who likely never existed. They lived (or, in Expedite's case, was supposed to have lived) within a century of each other. Both led aggressively un-Christian early lives before reforming themselves. But it is revealing that Augustine—the one who postponed change for such an agonizingly long time, who was racked with guilt over his behavior, who wrote with such impassioned regret—is the one who in the end proved so deeply influential, the one whose ideas are studied and whose works are read nearly two thousand years after his death.

The other, Expedite, was resolute and certain and heroic in stomping out the temptation in his life. As only a fictional figure could be.

Portraits of Expedite always show him in his Roman soldier's togs, carrying a cross and stepping on his nemesis, the crow. The vanquished bird holds in his beak a scroll bearing the Latin word for tomorrow, *CRAS*, the root of the English word "procrastination" and a close approximation of the sound of a crow's distinctive croak. The cross Expedite holds in his portraits reads *HODIE*—Latin for "today." There could be no plainer picture of the ascendancy of the immediate over the deferred, action over delay. The crow never had a chance.

Expedite's crow is a cousin to other literary and legendary birds: trickster ravens in Norse and Native American myth, for example, and poet Ted Hughes's mythic crows for another. The Hughes poem that most directly tackles delay and deferral isn't about crows. It's called "Thrushes," and in it the title birds are portrayed as nothing less than automatic killing machines. Spared the irresolution and the procrastination that plagues humans (like the dawdling poet), they are portrayed as single-minded, instinctual, ruthless.

Because Hughes's bird is more efficient than the poet, it is represented as a more complete creature. (Completeness is a big deal in the Old Testament, too, where the laws governing warfare issued in Deuteronomy command that the warrior who has not yet harvested his vineyard or finished building his home is unfit to fight for his people.) There is no romanticism about Hughes's bird, there are no pretty songs heralding the dawn. Hughes offers a more biologically accurate version of bird-dom—single-minded, untroubled, and therefore more terrible. Contra Emily Dickinson, Hughes's thing with feathers is death.

Death is the one obligation that cannot be postponed or procrastinated away. Edgar Allan Poe's "The Raven" stars another talking member of the species *Corvus*, and like

Expedite's crow, the bird is described as a "tempter," "devil," and "fiend"—and most relevantly, one that won't go away no matter how many times he is asked. But in Poe's poem, unlike the St. Expedite legend, the avian herald of death wins the battle with the human he haunts. He remains perched "on the pallid bust of Pallas just above my chamber door" even after the speaker of the poem has succumbed.

Poe was himself a committed procrastinator. He wrote in a letter to the poet James Russell Lowell, "I am excessively slothful and wonderfully industrious by fits." His familiarity with the feast-and-famine work habits of the procrastinator helped him construct one of literature's most perfect renditions of the procrastinator's mind, in his story "The Imp of the Perverse."

We have a task before us which must be speedily performed. We know that it will be ruinous to make delay. The most important crisis of our life calls, trumpet-tongued, for immediate energy and action. We glow, we are consumed with eagerness to commence the work, with the anticipation of whose glorious result our whole souls are on fire. It must, it shall be undertaken to-day, and yet we put it off until to-morrow, and why? There is no answer, except that we feel perverse, using the word with no comprehension of the principle. To-morrow arrives, and with it a more impatient anxiety to do our duty, but with this very increase of anxiety arrives, also, a nameless, a positively fearful, because unfathomable, craving for delay. This craving gathers strength as the moments fly. The last hour for action is at hand. We tremble with the violence of the conflict within us,—of the definite with the indefinite—of the substance with the shadow. But, if the contest have proceeded thus far, it is the shadow which prevails,—we struggle in vain. The clock strikes, and is the knell of our welfare. At the same time, it is the chanticleer-note to the ghost that has so long overawed us. It flies—it disappears—we are free. The old energy returns. We will labor now. Alas, it is too late!

Poe's "too late" echoes Augustine's "too late." Like the saint, Poe was spiritually inclined toward regret. During his last years, stricken with grief over the death of his young wife, Virginia, Poe lived near a community of Jesuit priests in the Bronx and visited them at night, sometimes to use their library, but often to have dinner with them or to join in their games of cards. The depressed poet found consolation with the priests and wrote gratefully that they were "highly cultivated gentlemen and scholars, they smoked and they drank and they played cards and they never said a word about religions."

The priests looked after Poe. When the poet was overcome with grief, or with drink, or with some combination of the two, one of the Jesuits would walk him home. Some have wondered why the priests never tried to bring Poe to their faith, never offered him the sacraments. A sympathetic ear, a steadying hand on a wobbly walk home, yes, but never a word about religion. Poe died in mysterious circumstances in Baltimore in 1849. According to one story, his last words were "Lord, help my poor soul."

Expedite and Augustine and Poe suggest an alternative way of understanding procrastination. More than just a matter of mood or of irrational decision-making or of poor time management, procrastination can be a matter of life and death. All of us are aware of the clock ticking, of our time running out. But deep down we also hope that somehow, magically, the clock might make an exception in our case. When I was a kid, nothing scared me more than the idea of eternity. I used to sit up at night in bed trying to understand the concept. How could time go on *forever*? And, more important from the perspective of a self-absorbed preteen, what would happen to me? Nothing is more incomprehensible to a kid—and to some adults—than the idea of the world without him. It is an impossibility.

Eternal life scared me, too. Forget hell and the torment of the damned. What gave me the willies was the thought of my soul floating on through endless time. Endless time. This was supposed to be the big prize waiting for all of us. But just thinking about it was enough to make me break out in a sweat.

<hr />

I have never prayed to Expedite, but I share his devotees' optimism, their faith that good things will come. Procrastinators may be depressed, delusional, self-destructive, but we are also optimists; we believe that there will always be a better time than the present to do what needs to be done. Optimism is the quality most often overlooked in procrastinators. For us, tomorrow is always brimming with promise.

There can be something thrilling about delay. Maybe it is the thrill of transgression, the high that comes along with not doing what you are supposed to do when you are supposed to do it. There must be a reason, based in the principles of narrative presumably, that superheroes are always waiting until the last moment to arrive and save the day. Superheroes play out a secular version of religious conversion, transforming themselves from everyday, frail beings to other, more robust ones, while somehow remaining the same beings, all in service of producing some kind of salvation.

Augustine liked to portray mortal life itself as a pause; he called it "this delay from which I suffer." He considered it an irksome postponement of the eternal life waiting for believers. Augustine was impatient to get on with it. That's optimistic.

My optimism peaks almost immediately after I wake up. I've always liked mornings, and am less self-pitying, less of a pain in the ass then than at any other time of day. In the morning, anything seems possible. I am brimming with ideas! Potential! Love for others! I cannot be stopped. By four in the afternoon, I have given up entirely on myself and on humanity. This is why late afternoon is peak procrastination time. This is when, desperately, I give up on the day and invest everything in tomorrow. I have made a religion of bailing out of the present and living for tomorrow morning.

Belief in tomorrow is a species of faith: if I can only make it until tomorrow, it seems to me, everything will be new again, hope resurrected. For procrastinators, hope always triumphs over experience. I suppose that's a pretty workable definition of faith.

The day I finally got to meet Father Tony at Our Lady of Guadalupe, I found myself with a few minutes to kill, and so decided to duck into the church. It was about four in the afternoon, and a few blocks away on Bourbon Street, the partying was already well under way. On my way over, I passed a nightclub where, in the front door, stood a woman in hot pants with her companion, a muscle-shirted dude with tree-trunk arms and a ponderous gut. She called out to me, "Come party with us, honey." Something, maybe the presence of the dude in the muscle shirt, made me pretend I hadn't heard.

Inside Our Lady of Guadalupe, things were quieter. An elderly woman prayed a rosary near the altar. In the back of the church sat a few people who looked as if they might not have anywhere else to go, loitering in the pews. The church ticked in the heat. No one was paying much attention to St. Expedite.

In the early Christian church, it was almost universally expected that the Last Days and Final Judgment were imminent, around the corner, sure to come sooner rather than later. The expectation drove some people slightly crazy. Every few decades or so, a frenzied panic would overcome large groups of believers. Certain of the need to repent before it was too late, they gave away all they had, formed messianic mobs, walked across Europe to visit holy sites, and launched violent Crusades.

This kind of anxiety is not unique to believers. Who hasn't feared missing out, waiting too long, being left behind? Living with urgency requires belief in something, even if it is something no bigger than your insignificant self. The most religious question most of us ask is not "Why am I here?" but "How much longer do I have?"

It makes me think of a story Father Tony told me during my second visit to Our Lady of Guadalupe—one of those humorous, *Reader's Digest*-y anecdotes that Catholic priests like to sprinkle in their Sunday sermons to draw a few laughs and keep the congregation awake for a few more minutes: It seems one day a preacher asked his flock how many of them wanted to go to heaven. All in attendance raised their hands except one holdout. The preacher, peering out over the congregation, asked the lone exception if it was really true that he didn't want to go to heaven. The man responded, "Of course I want to go to heaven, Father. But it sounded like you were planning on making the trip *today*."

Augustine called his life "this delay from which I suffer" because he was ready to make his trip to paradise as soon as possible. Most of us aren't so sure. There is a native ambivalence about us that makes us resist even the most perfect thing.

Heaven sounds promising. But not yet.

4

|||||||||||

A BRIEF HISTORY
OF THE TO-DO LIST

Who would write who had anything better to do?

—LORD BYRON, IN HIS JOURNAL

The Italian writer Umberto Eco was obsessed with lists. Eco had been known only in academic circles, as a semiotician, until he wrote a hugely successful 1980 novel called *The Name of the Rose*. A Sherlock Holmes–ish story transplanted to fourteenth-century Italy with a monk (William of Baskerville) standing in for the detective, it was made into a lousy movie starring Sean Connery and Christian Slater. The book's success turned Eco into a very unlikely

---

71

celebrity. He was a celebrity who liked to read dictionaries. Once, when asked which book he would choose to keep him company in solitude on a desert island, he chose a telephone directory.

In a book called *The Infinity of Lists*, Eco suggested that lists are our only way to express the things that defy expression. In Homer's *Iliad*, the poet attempts to describe the Greek forces arrayed for the invasion of Troy, but gives up. Instead, he offers a list: the Catalogue of Ships, a 350-line roll call of the Greek commanders and their troops.

Eco said we are attracted to lists because of their infinitude. Lists have no limits and can never be complete. "We have a limit, a very discouraging, humiliating limit: death. That's why we like all the things that we assume have no limits, and therefore, no end. It's a way of escaping thoughts about death," Eco said. "We like lists because we don't want to die."

I am a slightly compulsive list-maker, but the one kind of list I have never made is a bucket list. I have never made a bucket list because I lack the physical courage to do many of the things that would qualify for a bucket list—I would never skydive or hang glide or run a marathon or climb Mount Everest, for example.

Bucket lists operate at the intersection of acquisitiveness and self-improvement; they reveal an urge to polish our résumés and pile up impressive experiences right to the very end. Credit for popularizing the term goes to Justin Zackham, who wrote the screenplay for the Jack Nicholson and Morgan Freeman film of the same name. The idea for the screenplay came from Zackham's own list of things he wanted to do before dying. You may have already guessed that number one on his list was to write a screenplay that would be produced by a major Hollywood studio.

The other reason I have never made a bucket list is that it requires acknowledging my own mortality and I am resolutely not in favor of acknowledging my own mortality. To complete a task is to make it disappear, and in some way, to make ourselves disappear, too. This also accounts for why I so often fail to complete my to-do lists. As long as I have things to do before me, preferably an infinitely unrealizable series of things, there is no limit to how long I can continue to put them off. What could be more discouraging than crossing off the last item on the last to-do list? I want the lists to go on forever—and me, too, if possible.

When I returned from New Orleans, I had a longish list of jobs waiting for me, some big, some small, and it was then that I finally saw the point of making oblations to St.

Expedite. The point is, of course, that it is helpful to have someone other than yourself to blame for not getting your work done. I had bought at least three prayer cards in the gift shop at Our Lady of Guadalupe, and still I was getting so very little done. Didn't this seem a little unfair? I understood better than ever all the decapitated Expedite figures on the roadsides of Réunion Island.

Meanwhile, I kept sliding deeper and deeper into a hole relative to my deadlines—a hole being a void, and avoiding being about the only thing I was doing about work right then. Tasks like updating my Twitter profile all of a sudden seemed more vitally important than anything else I could imagine. I spent most of one day editing my collection of digital music files. I think "curating" is the word used now.

The more I resolved to stay on task, the more unfocused I became. My inability to work depressed me and—you know how this works—my depression made it impossible for me to work. Entire workweeks passed in a fog of distraction and task avoidance. Searching for a quote in a book on my shelves, I would find a collection of music criticism that I had never gotten around to reading, and even though it wasn't at all what I was looking for, I would take it down, and before long I would be deep into a reconsideration of the New Zealand garage-pop scene of the 1980s.

And I would have totally forgotten what it was that I had gone looking for in the first place.

I knew I should stop procrastinating, and resolved to do so, but even in this regard I was too often guilty of what I suppose you could call meta-procrastination, in which my resolve to stop procrastinating evaporated and I ended up doing nothing about my tendency to do nothing.

Whenever I couldn't bring myself to do what I knew I should be doing, I made to-do lists. For me, and I bet for most procrastinators, the whole point of the to-do list is that it enhances the satisfaction in blowing something off. If you didn't first list the thing you are now putting off, you might not ever realize that you weren't doing that thing. And where is the fun in that?

I made lists of essays to be written, revisions to be completed, and e-mails to be sent or responded to. There were lists of magazine stories to be pitched and lists of editors to pitch them to. There were lists of bills to be paid, websites to be visited, errands to be run, laundry to be done, and depressed friends to be called and cheered up. By the end of a typical day, my workspace was like a library of lists. I left lists for myself on the desk, on the bed, and masking-taped to a cabinet.

Sometimes I lost my lists and found them only later. This was no problem. Even my weeks-old lists were usually still uncompleted, and in that sense, still perfectly good. Old lists were welcomed back, like sheep that had strayed, to join the rest of the herd.

It's nice to think that lists could be a way of ordering our chaotic lives, but my list-making has never had much to do with getting things done. Just the opposite. I love lists because list-making itself feels like an achievement, and therefore relieves me of the responsibility of achieving whatever goals I have set for myself on my list.

Making a list, managing a list, losing a list, then spending part of an afternoon looking for a lost list—these all take up some of the time that I might spend actually doing some of the things on that list. I suppose this is one of the reasons so many people are so addicted to to-do lists. The other is that making a list of things to be done is often more satisfying than actually doing the things on the list. Naming obligations is usually more fun than fulfilling them.

Wandering the Internet a while ago, ostensibly in the name of research, I came across a to-do list Johnny Cash is supposed to have at some point scrawled in a date book, under the heading "THINGS TO DO TODAY!"

1. Not Smoke
2. Kiss June
3. Not Kiss anyone else
4. Cough
5. Pee
6. Eat
7. Not eat too much
8. Worry
9. Go See Mama
10. Practice Piano

For a long time I wondered if the exclamation mark in the heading indicated a sunny optimism that I would not have anticipated from the Man in Black. Or did it merely suggest desperation?

But the item that really marks Cash as a genius among list makers is number 8: "Worry." Can anyone ever really worry enough? And, having worried enough, wouldn't one naturally start to worry that one has worried too much? Worry can never really be crossed off a list of things to do. It is a meta-ambition, an ambition entirely about itself and therefore one that can never be realized, because even having had it on one's list is cause for worry. It's dizzying, if you think about it long enough. It produces a kind of spiritual vertigo, a deep psychic discomfort that I think Cash must have known, because the item that follows "Worry" on his to-do list is "Go See Mama."

The greatest American list maker was Benjamin Franklin, who in the *Pennsylvania Gazette* of January 6, 1737, published a list of more than two hundred ways of saying that someone is drunk. ("He's got his Topgallant Sails out," for example.) Franklin is also credited with pioneering the use of lists of pros and cons as a decision-making tool. And when he was twenty, Franklin famously compiled a list of thirteen virtues (temperance, silence, order, etc.) to which he aspired. He meant for the list to function like a moral spreadsheet. He recorded his failings, marking "by a little black spot every fault I found by examination to have been committed" relating to each virtue. Franklin's idea was to master each virtue in turn until he had completed the list and achieved perfect virtue. He would live another sixty-four years, but Franklin at twenty was already in a hurry to succeed. "Dost thou love life? Then do not squander time, for that's the stuff life is made of," he wrote. And, "Lost time is never found again."

The American self-help industry can trace its origins to Franklin. Scholars debate whether Franklin himself was entirely serious about some of the advice he published, or whether he might have been spoofing the sort of sober Puritan moralism that is the foundation of the American way of work. It's easy to see why Franklin might be suspected of having some fun with his readers. He was enormously accomplished, a prolific inventor and writer, it's true; but he also spent an awful lot of time lying around in bathtubs, sometimes with one of his French mistresses. He was not so obsessed with productivity that he didn't know how to waste an afternoon.

One twentieth-century example of the American list-making, note-jotting, high-achieving type is Dwight Eisenhower, the general who chain-smoked his way through the exhaustive and meticulous planning of the Normandy invasion, but is now better remembered as a president who spent an inordinate portion of his two terms in the White House golfing. Like Franklin, Eisenhower has become an icon of American productivity. His reputation in this area originates from a speech he gave at Northwestern University in the late 1950s, in which he quoted a "retired college president" about how to make the most of any allotted reserve of time: "What is important is seldom urgent and what is urgent is seldom important." Eisenhower was probably quoting himself; he had been president of Columbia University after the war. Ironically, his brusque, militarily efficient management style alienated much of the faculty there, who were more comfortable with endless and aimless committee discussions.

But Eisenhower's quote attracted the attention of the writer and educator Stephen Covey, who would develop the FranklinCovey productivity business. Covey made the quote the basis of what came to be called the Eisenhower Matrix. A decision maker is supposed to divvy up his to-do list into four categories: do now; decide when to do it; delegate it; and delete it. This was meant to be an improvement on the to-do list, with the budgeting of time eliminating the kind of dicking around that philosopher Mark Kingwell has called action-as-inaction—the inconsequential busyness that makes it possible for us to not do what the world thinks we should be doing. My own suspicion is that many of the people you admire as devoted parents or selfless Scout troop leaders are doing their admirable deeds, at least partly, to avoid doing something else—like, for example, their jobs.

Most of us recognize that sometimes inaction can be a kind of action. The Symbolist poet Saint-Pol-Roux posted a notice on his bedroom door each night before going to bed: "Do not disturb. The poet is working." That's a little precious, but it nods toward our understanding that results come not just from constant effort, busyness, and motion, but also from repose, meditativeness, and receptivity.

As a procrastinator, I know how to make this human need for inaction work for me. I let myself read one more book, listen to Coltrane, take a shower or a walk around the park, and it all gets filed under "writing." As in, *I know it looks like I'm lying here with a drink in my hand staring vacantly at the ceiling, but I'm really writing.* At some point, you tell yourself, you will stop "writing" and start writing.

So much of my procrastination begins with anxiety. I worry that a magazine piece I have been assigned is beyond my abilities, and so I put off work on it. I worry that some long-needed household repair will turn out to be even more complicated and more costly than I had thought, so I delay that, too. I worry that my doctor will find something wrong with me, something I'd really rather not think about, and so year after year, I put off seeing him. So many things to do, so many reasons to worry, so many lists.

In 1482 Leonardo da Vinci wrote to Ludovico Sforza, regent of Milan, looking for employment. Leonardo had a sense for what would matter most to the badass ruler of one of Italy's warring city-states, so in his job letter he listed his many capabilities: construction of catapults and other siege weapons; design of portable bridges with which to "pursue and at any time flee from the enemy"; Leonardo had even worked out plans for a "covered chariot," a war vehicle that sounds a lot like a predecessor to a modern tank.

It was only at the very end of the letter that Leonardo mentioned that he could paint.

Leonardo's pitch letter worked. But upon hiring him, Ludovico put him to work not on any military project, but on a massive bronze sculpture called the *Gran Cavallo*. A monument to the duke's father, it was to be the world's largest equestrian statue. Like so many other Leonardo projects, it never quite reached completion. The problem of casting such an enormous work in one piece may have stymied Leonardo; his work on it stalled for years. At some point Ludovico must have tired of waiting for its completion. When French troops threatened Milan, and the city's defenders found themselves wanting firepower, Ludovico appropriated the bronze set aside for Leonardo's horse for use in casting artillery.

The cycle of ambitious promise and frustrating delay was standard operating procedure for Leonardo. He had a head full of ideas, but was constantly harried by noble folk wanting portraits. Leonardo was famous in his own time for making big plans, then never getting around to realizing them. He had his own agenda. He was constantly setting enormous tasks for himself, and he maintained a remarkably ambitious to-do list: "Describe how clouds are formed and how they dissolve" was one chore typical of those he listed. "Describe what sneezing is," another. And like a lot of the contract workers I know, he seemed to not like saying no to new assignments, which may be why he left so many works unfinished. His first biographer, Giorgio Vasari, suggested that it was Leonardo's perfectionism that got in the way: "He began many things [but] it appeared to him that the hand was not able to attain the perfection of art in executing the things which he imagined." Pope Leo X, frustrated by Leonardo's tardiness, is said to have declared, "This man will accomplish nothing."

Today we are amazed by Leonardo's sketches for helicopters, submarines, and robots, but in his time his patrons mostly wanted to know when he would finally finish the portraits he had promised.

Leonardo completed only twenty paintings in his lifetime, and two of those share the same name: *The Virgin of the Rocks*. This anomaly came about because in 1483 Milan's Confraternity of the Immaculate Conception asked Leonardo to produce a painting of the Virgin Mary and Christ Child for an altarpiece in their chapel. With a naive optimism familiar to anyone who has ever made a living as a contract worker, Leonardo agreed to finish the project in seven months. It would be twenty-five years before Leonardo's painting was installed.

The delay has landed Leonardo on a lot of lists of history's most famous procrastinators. Leonardo himself, late in his life, is said to have agonized over all he had left undone.

But can his procrastination really be separated from his genius? We value him today as a polymath, a thinker who bounded from art to anatomy to astronomy to engineering, making important advances in each field. The failings that frustrated his contemporaries make him seem distracted and capricious. But isn't it possible that a more workmanlike Leonardo, one who cared only about pleasing his patrons and meeting deadlines, would have done nothing worth re-membering?

That's the kind of argument that appeals to procrasti-nators, providing cover for our tendency to delay. But the history is more complicated. Leonardo produced his paint-ing for the Chapel of the Immaculate Conception with relative dispatch—only a couple of years late. But, insulted by the meager payment offered for the work, he held on to it to spite his patrons, then sold it to someone else. That painting, which never made it to the chapel, now hangs in the Louvre.

Chastened, the Confraternity eventually made Leonardo a second offer, which he accepted, thus committing himself to a second go at the work. This one took him fifteen years to finish. (Or as one circumspect source put it, "Execution of the commission was protracted.") This second version of *The Virgin of the Rocks*, which you can see at London's National Gallery, if you can push your way through the crowds, finally fulfilled Leonardo's contract with the Confraternity, who installed it behind the altar in 1508, a quarter century after Leonardo had promised to deliver it in seven months.

Procrastinators, according to the strictest definition of the term, choose to delay knowing that delaying will probably come back to bite them later. So if procrastination involves acting (or not acting) contrary to my own self-interest, the question that has to be asked is What sort of person acts against what he thinks is his own self-interest? The ancient Greeks (of course) had a word for this behavior. They called it *akrasia:* willfully acting against one's better judgment. Socrates argued that genuinely akratic behavior was impossible because no one who fully understood what was best for him would fail to do what was best for him. "No one goes willingly toward the bad," he argued.

Aristotle, on the other hand, believed that *akrasia* accurately described a failure of the will. Appetites or passions overtake reason: I genuinely want to get in shape, but I don't because, instead of exercising, I choose to watch *Talladega Nights* on Hulu and eat a pint of Häagen-Dazs salted caramel ice cream. So I get the pleasure of the pint of Häagen-

Dazs, but forfeit the fitness. I didn't do what I believed was best for me.

Akratic behavior shouldn't be all that hard to understand, given that we seem to be wired to satisfy certain animal appetites that may not be good for us—a night with the wrong person, a long afternoon at the corner tap, that pint of salted caramel ice cream. We know it's not healthy, we know it's not rational, but we do it anyway, and then we feel really bad about it. We think we've been less than human, as some of our idioms suggest: we've made a pig of ourselves, we say, or we've been complete asses. Maybe we get sick as a dog as a result. The sixteenth-century poet Edmund Spenser named the sorceress in *The Faerie Queene* Acrasia. She had the power to turn her lovers into animals. They couldn't control themselves.

It happens to the brightest of us. The Nobel Prize–winning economist George Akerlof wrote a 1991 paper called "Procrastination and Obedience" that begins with an anecdote about Akerlof's continued failure, day after day, to send a package from India, where he was living, to the United States, where his friend and colleague Joseph Stiglitz was waiting for it. "Each morning for over eight months, I woke up and decided that the next morning would be the day to send the Stiglitz box," Akerlof wrote. But each morning for over eight months, the box remained where it was.

This is comforting, on one level: it's nice to know that even brilliant scholars procrastinate. On the other hand, if you are the kind of person who is baffled by procrastination, you may want to shake Akerlof by the lapels: *Just mail the damn box!* Akerlof, too, was struck by the mystery. In procrastination, he saw evidence that our judgment and decision-making, contrary to the assumptions of classical economics, were ruled by impulses that were less than entirely rational. Akerlof's field, behavioral economics, studies how real, occasionally irrational people make real, occasionally irrational decisions.

One of the specific categories of irrationality mastered by procrastinators is what economists call hyperbolic discounting—the tendency to value immediate rewards (smaller ones that come sooner) over those we have to wait for (larger and later). Thus, a graduate student puts off working on a dissertation that will increase his chances of getting a decent job one day so that he can play another game of online Scrabble. He is favoring his present self over his future self. Let's leave aside for now the possibility that the procrastinating grad student, by wasting time playing online Scrabble, is really articulating a lack of faith that the promised big payoff (a decent job) will ever be forthcoming.

Procrastination is possible only in a world where choice is a paramount value, like our global consumerist swap-meet of an economy. The free market is supposed to be essential to human liberty, and choice one of our most treasured rights. But if you are like me and have ever spent long, agonized minutes in the cereal aisle of a supermarket, unable to pick between Honey Smacks and Cap'n Crunch, you know that choice can also be a burden that weighs heavily.

Doubt is a product of a choice. Should I accept this job? Should I paint my bedroom blue? Should I ask this person to marry me? Should I go see a doctor about this thing on my shoulder that won't go away? I'm not sure; I can't decide. I wake up, like Akerlof, knowing there are certain things I should do today. But which, exactly? A to-do list is a menu, and in the depths of procrastination, what I really want is for the waiter to tell me what to order.

⸻

Leonardo never finished his *Gran Cavallo*. He did manage a twenty-four-foot-tall clay model of the horse in 1493, but it was soon destroyed by archers who used it for target practice. After Sforza, under threat of invasion, repurposed Leonardo's eighty tons of bronze as raw material for cannon shot, the plans for the enormous horse were forgotten for centuries. Leonardo's design turned up again only when some of his old notebooks were uncovered in Madrid in 1965. An American art collector named Charles Dent read about the aborted project in an issue of *National Geographic* and decided to fund a second attempt. The sculptor he hired, Nina Akamu, finally completed a version of Leonardo's monumental horse. It wasn't exactly the monument Leonardo had designed, but it was twenty-five feet tall and weighed fifteen tons. It was unveiled in Milan in 1999, five hundred years after Leonardo's clay model had been destroyed.

I like to think of it as a monument to the procrastinator's battle with himself. Be patient. Someone, somewhere, even if it is five hundred years after the fact, may finish the things you never got around to doing.

| | | | | | | | | | |

5

ON THE CLOCK

We do not want any initiative. All we want of them is to obey the orders we give them, do what we say, and do it quick.

—FREDERICK WINSLOW TAYLOR,
LECTURING ON MANAGEMENT, 1907

Among the laborers at Massachusetts's Watertown Arsenal in the summer of 1911, there was one nearly universal source of complaint: a wellborn management consultant named Frederick Winslow Taylor. For nearly three years, Taylor and his aides had been stalking the arsenal, stopwatches in hand, timing workers at their various jobs in an attempt to improve the workers' efficiency and eliminate wasted time. Turner hoped to discover and dictate an optimal, standardized time for the completion of every task undertaken in the plant, from sharpening tools to hauling materials to pouring the molds for the big coastal defense guns made there.

This was how Taylor made his living: he watched people work, measured the pace of their work as precisely as he could (which was not always so precisely), then wrote a long report to their bosses about how these people could do their jobs better and more quickly.

The workingmen of the arsenal called him Speedy.

The U.S. Army had hired Taylor to streamline the manufacturing operations at the arsenal, which turned out carriages for large seacoast cannon and field mortars. Taylor was already the go-to efficiency expert for industrialists hoping to maintain control of their increasingly complex businesses and, of course, maximize profits. He may have been the first of a species that would proliferate in the twentieth century: the high-priced, hotshot management consultant.

Born to a wealthy Philadelphia family, Taylor followed an eccentric path. Though he had been admitted to Harvard, the young Taylor instead took a job on the shop floor of a Philadelphia pump manufactory, rising to the position of machinist and ultimately chief engineer at the Midvale Steel

Company in Nicetown, Pennsylvania. At the same time, he distinguished himself as an upper-crust club sportsman. He and a partner won a tennis doubles championship at the first U.S. Nationals in 1881 (where he used a racket of his own design); he later took fourth place in golf at the 1900 Olympics.

A gentleman not afraid to roll up his sleeves and sweat, Taylor was nevertheless miserable in his work. The problem was that his efforts to cajole more work out of the men beneath him earned him their contempt. Taylor was sensitive enough to be bothered by this. "It is a horrid life for any man to live, not to be able to look any workman in the face all day long without seeing hostility there," he confessed.

During his sabbatical on the shop floor, Taylor came to recognize a problem where no one before had seen one: the tremendous variability in ways of accomplishing a simple task. Take, for example, shoveling sand. Sand shovelers might do their shoveling with their own tools, using their own techniques and at their own pace, which meant that there could be no uniformity of progress among workers assigned the same task. One sand shoveler might shovel much more sand than another sand shoveler, even though both sand shovelers were ostensibly tasked with the same mission, were to be compensated equally, and therefore might presumably be expected to shovel roughly equivalent quantities of sand.

Taylor noticed something else, too. Workforces tended to accommodate themselves to the pace of their slowest, most leisurely workers. Even a sand shoveler capable of shoveling a great deal of sand might not shovel at his most ambitious pace, for fear of showing up his fellow sand shovelers. Taylor called this phenomenon soldiering and said it was nearly universal.

Soldiering is related to procrastination, in that the soldierer sabotages the efforts of the collective the way a procrastinator frustrates himself. Reading Taylor's scathing descriptions of "mentally sluggish" workers soldiering on the job, I couldn't help but recognize myself. In retrospect, I could see that soldiering had been so much a part of my work life that I probably should have been wearing fatigues most of the time. At the grocery store where I worked in high school, it was understood that you didn't stack apples at too rapid a pace; it would set a dangerous precedent. Carting out debris for the renovator who employed me in college, I figured out that working at too rapid a pace would only be rewarded with more wheelbarrow loads.

Speedy Taylor would have been horrified by either of these operations. But he was right about the ubiquity of soldiering. The urge to defy bosses, to loaf, to perversely do what we damn well know we shouldn't be doing (or more relevantly, to *not* do what we damn well know we *should* be doing) is present in most jobs, especially those in which a workforce wants to flip management a metaphoric middle finger. In some contexts, soldiering may even be heroic, a variety of resistance. Some African slaves in the American South were known to disrupt or delay projects by moving at a shuffling pace, rather than conspire with the evil of chattel slavery. Some even poisoned themselves.

Radical dissents from late capitalism and consumerism are part of this history, too. The philosopher Guy Debord, the leading figure of the situationist movement, is most famous for a bit of writing that appeared not in a book, nor in a scholarly journal, but scrawled on a wall in the rue de Seine in 1953: *Ne Travaillez Jamais* (Never Work).

Debord really never did work. One of the things I learned when I looked into Debord's biography is that his first wife supported him for a time by "writing horoscopes for racehorses." It doesn't sound like a promising career, but if you're really set against working, career advancement doesn't really matter, does it?

Not working was no mere matter of laziness for Debord. He saw it as an assault on order. (He also had one of his early books, *Mémoires*, bound in sandpaper so that it would damage neighboring books on a shelf.) Maybe you want to dismiss Debord and the situationists as anachronistic, typical of a certain radical moment in history. But parts of their ethic remain relevant even for the most unquestioning capitalist today. Take the situationist *derive*—an unplanned and aimless stroll through urban space in which obligations are ignored and chance leads an adventurer from new encounter to new encounter. Take away the walking, and the *derive* shares many elements—the chance connections seized upon, the curiosity indulged, the time wasted—of an afternoon spent jumping from link to link on the Internet.

Taylor's claims of analytical rigor in studying work were taken very seriously by the leading minds of the time. The future Supreme Court justice Louis Brandeis was a big fan of Taylor's and in 1910 came up with the term "scientific management" to describe a school of thought that included not only Taylor but also Frank and Lillian Gilbreth, pioneers of motion study. The Gilbreths even applied statistical rigor to raising a family. Their regimented approach to raising their twelve children inspired the book and film *Cheaper by the Dozen*.

The assumption behind Taylor's analysis was laid out in his 1903 treatise *Shop Management:* Workers could not be trusted to perform their tasks competently on their own (they were, remember, "mentally sluggish" and "naturally lazy") but needed direction from managers who could dictate a standardized, optimal technique and pace for any task. There was "one best way" to do any job—that was the phrase that came to be associated with Taylorism and efficiency—and it was up to management to discover that best way and impose it on the workforce.

At Midvale, Taylor had worked in the machine shop, where enormous, belt-driven machines cut steel locomotive tires to size. Taylor had studied the operation of the machines and broken the whole metal-cutting operation down to variables—the shape of the tool, the speed of the setting, the variety of metal—that could be quantified and reduced to equations workable on a slide rule. He wanted to bring a similarly machinelike efficiency to human operations. He saw his mission as a noble one and himself as a visionary, using science to bring opportunity and enlightenment to the laboring classes.

In fact, Taylor's analyses were not really all that scientific. At Bethlehem Steel, where he was hired in 1898, he determined the best rate for loading pig iron by selecting "twelve large, powerful Hungarians" and challenging them to load sixteen and a half tons of iron as quickly as they could. It took them fourteen minutes. Then Taylor started tweaking the numbers, subjecting them to such formulae as the "law of heavy laboring," which posited the ideal work-

to-rest ratio. (Hint: it's a lot to a little.) A little more manip-
ulation of the data, and Taylor had his conclusion: a properly
motivated—and constantly supervised—worker could load
seventy-one tons per day.

Science, such as it was, had spoken. This figure was installed as the new standard at Bethlehem. To provide an
incentive, Taylor set higher wages for those who were able
to meet the standard. Those who refused to play along with
the system were dismissed.

The workers, mostly recent immigrants, grumbled in-
cessantly about Taylor and his college-boy aides trying to
tell them how to do their work—just as the grunts later
would grumble at Watertown. At the arsenal, laborers
were especially touchy because they regarded Taylor's scientific management as an affront to their contributions to
the nation's defense. It threatened their very patriotism.
The striking molders there wrote in a petition that Taylor's
methods were "humiliating to us, who have always tried to
give the Government the best that was in us. This method
is un-American."

The strike at the arsenal lasted only a week, ending with
the reinstatement of a worker who had been dismissed for
balking at Taylor's dictates. But it prompted an investigation
by the Labor Committee of the U.S. House of Representa-

tives, giving Taylor an opportunity to explain his methods to the nation. It did not go well.

"I can say, without the slightest hesitation," Taylor told the committee, "that the science of handling pig-iron is so great that the man who is . . . physically able to handle pig-iron and is sufficiently phlegmatic and stupid to choose this for his occupation is rarely able to comprehend the science of handling pig-iron."

When he compared a worker who would not meet his dictated time standards to "a bird that can sing but won't sing," one furious congressman responded, "We are not dealing with horses nor singing birds but with men who are part of society and for whose benefit society is organized."

As a result of its investigation, Congress banned the use of stopwatches to time workers in factories.

Congress's disapproval notwithstanding, Taylor's ideas took root. The same year as the Watertown strike, Taylor published *The Principles of Scientific Management,* a volume that would become the best-selling business book of the first half of the twentieth century. It can be considered a precursor to every business-success book found in every airport book kiosk today. Peter Drucker very enthusiastically called it "the most powerful as well as the most lasting contribution America has made to Western thought since the

Federalist Papers." Drucker placed Taylor alongside Freud and Darwin in a trio of thinkers responsible for the modern world. Taylor himself settled for calling his ideas "a mental revolution."

He wasn't wrong. Taylor's ideas influenced Henry Ford as he developed his assembly-line systems. They also appealed to national leaders as disparate as Mussolini and Lenin. The *Rationalisierung,* or rationalization, of Weimar Germany made Taylorist efficiency and order the basis of an entire economy. Mitsubishi and other Japanese corporations embraced Taylorism as early as the 1920s and never let up in their admiration. When Taylor's son visited Japan in the 1960s, executives from Toshiba begged him for pictures of his father, and for anything—a pencil perhaps?—once handled by the great man.

A little skepticism about glib historical analogy is almost always warranted, but it's not hard to see Taylor's influence in our current attitudes about work, time, and productivity. "Budgeting our time," as we are advised, means thinking about time in an economic sense, as a resource to be stewarded, marshaled, deployed wisely. (Isn't it remarkable how much of our language concerning time is also the language of money? We spend time, waste time, save time, lose time.) To say that time is money is to employ cliché, but there really isn't a more concise distillation of Taylor's philosophy.

Taylor is the Ur-source of our obsession with productivity and efficiency in both personal and professional lives—though I'm not sure it still makes sense to refer to the two spheres as separate. To the extent that we are always aware of the clock ticking, to the extent that we feel there is never enough time for us to do the things we think need to be done, to the extent that we are all multitasking and writing memos to ourselves and moving from chore to chore as dictated by the pinging of an iPhone, we are living the legacy of Taylorism.

The critic Louis Menand has written about how ideas about "best practices" have a tendency to move from business schools to the general culture. The result is that we end up internalizing some ideal of personal competence that has little to do with the way people really live. We evaluate ourselves by the standards of this managed ideal and of course we are found wanting. We fail our own annual review.

We have been yoking the personal to the professional at least since the dawn of self-help. Even the first work of that genre, Samuel Smiles's *Self-Help*, depicts professional life as requiring total and constant commitment. Here's Menand on Smiles: "One striking thing about the exemplary tales in *Self-Help* is the all-consuming nature of the careers they document. There is no separation between work life and private life. Personal prosperity and professional success coincide, and this elision became a staple of the genre. The secrets of success in business are the secrets of success in life." One of those secrets, of course, is to maximize time as one would any precious resource. Thus, procrastination, a dysfunction in our relationship with time, is an obstacle to success. Only the truly self-defeating have no economy of time—they don't save, it, don't spend it wisely, don't budget it. They kill it.

I suppose my initial reaction, as I read more and more deeply into Taylor, was predictable: the reflexive disdain of a humanist for any authoritarian, data-driven program. But then something funny happened. I began to develop an appreciation for Speedy Taylor and his stopwatches. Anyone who has ever been plagued by indecision will know that sometimes what you want is someone to tell you what to do. I have spent enough of my life dithering, vacillating between this option and that, and ultimately doing neither, that I could see the advantage of having some stopwatch-wielding authority figure to save me from my self-sabotage.

Of course, only someone who doesn't actually have to

contend with a looming, stopwatch-wielding authority figure would be dense enough to think this way. If I did have such a person telling me what to do I would rebel as readily as Taylor's steelworkers. Schedules imposed on me restrict my options. It's not that I think defying those schedules—procrastinating—is necessarily heroic. Just totally human.

In Bruce Beresford's film *Black Robe*, Jesuit missionaries in New France teach their Huron students to heed the orders of "Captain Clock," literally a chiming timepiece that will tell them when to study, when to eat, when to pray. In one scene, when the clock chimes the hour, the Huron excitedly say, "Captain Clock is speaking!" Their excitement is rooted in a theology that gives the clock face the job of expressing the will of God.

Now that job goes to other devices: the Fitbit that tallies miles walked, the app that measures calories consumed. All the alerts, alarms, pings, and pokes that tell us what to do and when to do it might as well be updated versions of Taylor's standardization program. For us, too, Captain Clock is speaking.

I had started to worry about my work habits. By which I mean that I worried about my habit of not getting to work.

There were some days when I felt a Taylor-like contempt for my own sluggishness. There were some days when entire hours, entire afternoons, slipped by, lost to coffee-making and texting and reading Wikipedia entries on jazz bassists.

I started most days with good intentions, but invariably became distracted or discouraged or otherwise knocked off track. Another day would slip away, unseized. Wasn't there some way I could end this habit of squeezing my workday down to a sliver that slipped so easily through the cracks?

I know I'm not the only one wrestling with this problem. Days seem to be escaping from us, as if our lives have sprung a leak, and the most common complaint one hears from a certain kind of professional-class complainer is that there just isn't enough time for all that cries out to be done. Our offspring, voracious and relentless in their demands on our time, get a certain amount of blame for this situation. So do our jobs, which have expanded, bloblike, from the old punch-the-clock, *Leave It to Beaver*-esque, nine-to-five routine to today's state of siege, with e-mails from the boss reaching us at night, in bed, just as we are starting to nod off.

The revolutionary connectivity of the Internet was supposed to let us work faster, smarter, better—and maybe it does, sometimes. But technology, of course, is also really good at distracting us. You know the drill. You sit down with your coffee, to work through your overnight e-mail. Inbox Zero beckons. You see that someone has sent you a link that demands your attention. This first link leads very quickly to a second. And while the first link had at least a tenuous claim on relevance to your professional duties, the second is wholly recreational, which is to say, much more irresistible. And there is always another link to follow, always more bait to bite at, always another carnivalesque headline ("16 Celebrity Yoga Pants Fails That You MUST See!") to click on.

When you come up for air it is lunchtime, somehow.

Still ahead is the hollow afternoon feeling of listlessness and exhaustion that comes with this routine. This feeling is cousin to what used to be called acedia—an inability to take interest in the world. Our immersive technologies have left us, literally, to our own devices.

At one point my friend Laura, hearing about my troubles and wanting to help, commandeered my laptop, so that she could "reconfigure my settings." Laura is as productive as I am dawdling, so I was willing to follow her lead. She set my computer so that I would be alerted to new messages less often, thus presumably reducing the risk of distraction. A good idea, I'm sure, but the truth is, this business of resetting my settings was deflating. It reduced what I liked to see as an existential crisis to something more along the lines of an IT interface problem. Could it be that all my soul-searching and self-doubt would really be ameliorated simply by resetting my settings? It was as if the world's most vexed insomniac had gone to see a doctor, only to be told to drink a glass of warm milk before going to bed each night.

In this effort to improve my work habits Laura also set my computer to announce the time, at every half hour, in a voice that sounded a little like Stephen Hawking's speech-generation device. "It's two o'clock," Not–Stephen Hawking would declare, and then what seemed like just a few seconds later, during which time I might have done nothing better than look at online photos of adorable corgis, Not–Stephen Hawking would announce, "It's two thirty." Taken together, the message of all these automated proclamations was clear: "Another day is dying. You are failing." I found that I was reliving on a daily basis the old end-of-weekend dread of my school days, when Sunday afternoon would dwindle into Sunday night, the promise of another weekend fading, re-placed by the looming dread of school's soul-killing obliga-tions. Not–Stephen Hawking didn't really motivate me to get to work, but he did make me want to throw my laptop out the window.

One of the problems may have been that at around this same time, I was using a Fitbit as a kind of digital task-master that measured how far I walked each day and how many calories I burned. This seemed like a good idea, except that my wife also bought a Fitbit and the two of us are very competitive, and so we became obsessed with outwalking each other. Each day I added more and more steps to my daily circuit, and made sure to tell my wife how many more steps I had added, thinking that this information would impress her. But of course she, too, had added steps to *her* daily routine, often more steps than I had added, and so I was compelled to walk even farther. It was like a cold war for pedestrians—mindless escalation sprung from insecurity. Entire days I spent in an exhausting pursuit of distance, which really didn't leave a lot of time for other activities, including work. None of the important things I had to do at the time mattered more to me than defeating my wife in our FitBit Pace-Off. Those other obligations, I decided, would just have to wait. I had miles to go before I could do what I should have been doing.

I guess you could call it ironic that my FitBit, which I had hoped would introduce a Taylor-esque discipline to my workday, instead ended up abetting my tendency to procrastinate. But I don't want to give the FitBit too much credit here, or too much blame, for that matter. The truth is that if I make up my mind to procrastinate, I don't need any kind of device to justify the impulse. I am, like so many of us, a powerfully self-motivated shirker.

It is a challenge for any procrastinator to live in our world of digital alerts, pokes, and nudges, all reminding us of some duty or other. These are examples of what people who think about these sorts of things call the extended will. The phrase refers to strategies to goad ourselves or trick ourselves into activity. The strategies may be psychological, like the bundling of tasks to pair an activity you like with one you loathe: thinking about how much money you are making while you endure the tedium of your cubicle, for example. Other strategies are environmental, like the construction of "chutes" to propel you into a task: setting out everything you need the night before for a first-thing-in-the-morning run, for example.

The need for an extended will suggests that plain, old-fashioned will is not quite up to the job. Willpower doesn't enjoy the currency it once did, maybe because so much social-science research demonstrates how lousy we are at controlling ourselves. (Does it not seem that there is now an entire sector of the American academy devoted to quantifying exactly what research subjects will do to get an extra cookie or a bonus marshmallow? Call it the Marshmallow Industrial Complex.)

It is nice to think that you could just will yourself to do what needs to be done. But it turns out there are a couple of problems with willpower. As the psychologist Roy

Baumeister has suggested, willpower can be thought of as a muscle that responds to regular use and atrophies when neglected. Thus, your willpower may or may not be prepared to help you when called upon. And what about all those *other* free wills out there, some of them in competition with *my* free will, determined to obstruct it? My will, in turn and without even meaning to, ends up colliding with theirs. The end result is that just about no one gets to do what they really want to do.

Some of the first public clocks appeared on priapic towers that rose in towns on the Italian peninsula in the 1300s. They were the product of an intense competition among emerging city-states for power, prestige, trade, and money. Any city aspiring to prominence had to have a public clock—and the bigger, taller, and louder, the better. The competition spawned an intercivic contest to build clock towers taller and more impressive than any others. Even now you can find at least a half dozen Italian cities that claim "the most beautiful clock in Italy."

This new time-telling technology was quickly adapted to the purposes of employers. So it was in fourteenth-century Italy that business owners first deployed clocks as a means to regulate the working lives of their employees. The marble quarry near Lake Maggiore, where workers cut away at stone for Milan's cathedral amid the voluptuous scents of the adjacent lemon groves, got its own clock in 1418. It controlled the working day of the laborers there, just as other clocks ruled the prayer life of the monks in their monasteries and the business day of the rising merchant class in town.

This is also when clocks began to tell us what we were worth. From the beginning, these rising towers enabled a new attitude toward time and the need to deploy it wisely. The one in Siena's Piazza del Campo, the Torre del Mangia, was supposedly named after a lazy bell ringer nicknamed Mangiaguadagni, "the profit eater," or the eater of time. The cautionary tale goes that Mangiaguadagni's profligacy cost him his job; to replace him, the tower was soon fitted with a mechanical brass ringer. He may have been the first worker in history to lose his job in the name of greater, mechanized productivity.

Like the disgruntled arsenal workers at Watertown, most of us recognize that to conform to dictated timelines and schedules is to cede some measure of individuality and humanity. Most of us also recognize that getting along in the world requires the occasional compromise. The things we do, the things we put off doing, the things we plan to do someday—these all define us, even if we don't fully under-stand why we are doing or not doing them.

It was only a few decades after clock towers began rising all over Italy that the procrastinating, deadline-shattering Leonardo sketched his *Vitruvian Man*, an effort to define and depict an ideally proportioned human. Leonardo's ideal man is shown inside a circle, arms raised.

He looks like nothing so much as a clock.

6

SEEDS

Cras melior est.

—MOTTO OF THE LICHTENBERGIAN SOCIETY

In the last decades of the eighteenth century, strollers on the streets of Göttingen in Lower Saxony became accustomed to seeing a man on the top floor of a half-timbered house on the Gotmarstrasse peering down at them as they walked. This was Georg Christoph Lichtenberg, one of the intellectual superstars of Enlightenment Europe.

A sensationally popular lecturer and showman of the sciences at the University of Göttingen in the 1760s, Lich-

tenberg was an eighteenth-century version of today's globe-
trotting academic luminaries: member of an intellectual
circle that included Goethe, Kant, and Alessandro Volta;
stager of science demonstrations that drew students and
admirers from around Europe; chummy conversational
partner to the king of England. If there had been TED
Talks in the Enlightenment, Lichtenberg probably would
have been pacing the stage in a periwig and wireless headset.

Lichtenberg was tiny and humpbacked and also something of a rock star. His lectures were routinely packed with
visitors who had traveled to Göttingen to see him. He was
hired at the university not only for his scientific abilities, but
also because the administration hoped that his charisma,
reputation, and showmanship would attract other scholars.

His life seemed to overflow with ideas and enthusiasms.
That overflow could be problematic. Lichtenberg never
seemed able to focus his energies. Or was it that Lichtenberg
wasn't interested in focusing? Again and again, Lichtenberg
did work that laid a foundation for new breakthroughs, only
to leave the breaking through to others. Lichtenberg demonstrated the scientific basis for hot-air balloon flight years
before the Montgolfier brothers were able to achieve the
first actual balloon flight. He himself never tried to leave
the ground.

Lichtenberg spoke often of writing a novel in the style

of Henry Fielding's *Tom Jones*. But there never seemed to be time. There were always lectures to give, letters to write, strolls to take. At his death, at fifty-six, Lichtenberg had finished only a few pages of his novel.

He dabbled. The wide scope of Lichtenberg's intellectual curiosity was part of his appeal, part of his genius. He lectured on astronomy and mathematics and geodesy and volcanology and meteorology and experimental physics. He authored an extended art-critical analysis of the prints of the English artist William Hogarth. He wrote short essays about what we would call psychology. Lichtenberg was sometimes frustrated by his own dabbling, by his failure to stick to the task at hand. The regret is unmistakable in one of his diary entries: "I had Montgolfier's invention within my reach," he wrote with the dismay of one smacking himself on the forehead.

Even in his achievements, you find traces of Lichtenberg's procrastination. One of his great discoveries in electrostatics came as a result of stepping away from his work one day to tidy up the scientific equipment in his laboratory—just the kind of task-avoidance any procrastinator would recognize. He had built an electrophorus, a metal disk about six feet in diameter, a device popularized by his friend Volta and used to generate an electrostatic charge. Probably seeking a reason—any reason—to put off work, he was one day moving things here and there around the laboratory and noticed that some dust on the disk had gathered in clusters, "like stars at certain points," he wrote. When he brushed the disk clean, the dust settled back into the same patterns. Charging the disk from a Leyden jar produced even funkier figures, like the product of an electrocharged Spirograph. Lichtenberg found that he could transfer the patterns from the disk onto paper.

He had stumbled upon the principle behind electrostatic printing. Lichtenberg figured out ways to manipulate powder into patterns, like an artist, to produce visually pleasing images. These he preserved under glass. Some of them still exist, and they look like the sorts of things you might find at a garage sale, in the dollar-and-under box. They would make really cool thank-you gifts. It wasn't until 1938 that Chester Carlson, with the advantage of two centuries' worth of subsequent advances, used Lichtenberg's discovery to develop xerography.

Lichtenberg's disinclination to focus his energies—let's go ahead and call it his procrastination—helps explain his relative obscurity as a figure in the history of science. In fact, insofar as Lichtenberg is remembered at all today, it is not as a scientist but as an aphorist. For thirty-four years, from 1765 to 1799, Lichtenberg jotted observations, one-liners, ephemera, and putdowns of hostile critics ("Whenever he composes a critical review, I have been told he gets an enormous erection . . .") in what he called *Sudelbücher,* or "waste books." The name referred to the eighteenth-century mercantile practice of recording notes of transactions in informal notebooks before transferring them into more durable and official ledgers. Lichtenberg filled his books with jottings, stray thoughts, and memoranda to himself. He never intended for any of it to be published. Yet they are what he is remembered for. Whatever claim on posterity he can make is based on the tossed-off witticisms in his *Waste Books*, which were published posthumously. They are said to have influenced latter-day essayists such as Susan Sontag and philosophers such as Ludwig Wittgenstein, whose late, aphoristic work displays a debt to Lichtenberg. Nietzsche, Kierkegaard, and Schopenhauer all would cite his Waste Books frequently and admiringly.

But the work Lichtenberg did publish and that made him notable in his time—his science, his travel writing, his art criticism—has been mostly forgotten.

Aphorism suited Lichtenberg. It is the ideal form for a procrastinator—flashes of insight presented with no need for further elaboration or development or argument. For the aphorist, elaboration would only foul everything up. Wittgenstein, who was, like Lichtenberg, prone to the gnomic, said that arguments just spoil the beauty of perceptions. Trying to prop up an insight with evidence was like dirtying a flower with muddy hands. That was the image Wittgenstein deployed. Better to leave it be.

Lichtenberg worked hard but never wanted to be *seen* to work hard. I get the feeling that he wasn't against achievement, but thought achievement worth pursuing only if it could be done with a certain style. He seemed to aim for an intellectual sprezzatura, a seeming carelessness that masks effort. If you have to show your work, it only ruins the effect of effortlessness.

Lichtenberg, like Wittgenstein, resorted to horticultural imagery in explaining his own work. He compared his jottings in The Waste Books to seeds, "which if they fall on the right soil may grow into chapters and even whole dissertations." Like seeds, they were small but rich with possibility. They had generative potential. They were not, as he saw them, significant works themselves, but might have significance stored within them.

So Lichtenberg's life is a paradox: He dabbled and dithered where he was supposed to be most diligent. But the work he thought too trifling to publish has proven durable and deeply influential. It has taken root.

In fairy tales, seeds become beanstalks that climb magically through clouds. They lead to danger, but also to treasure. When seeds are deployed as imagery they are usually standing in for an individual's moral choices and their consequences. Willy Loman's pathetic garden is an emblem of his hopelessness. Even Onan's Old Testament seed-spilling is punished as an act of betrayal of his own people. His tribe depends on his procreative power and that of all its men for its survival. In that context, spilling seed isn't perverse, it's criminally irresponsible, and so was condemned in much the same terms that procrastination is condemned.

Lichtenberg deplored his own procrastination, even while recognizing that it was necessary for him. He was ill for much of his life—or at least he *thought* he was. One observer called him "the Columbus of hypochondria." He wrote: "I have often daydreamed about all manner of fantastic things for hours on end, at times when people thought I was very busy. I saw the drawbacks of this as regards loss of time." But it was necessary. He called his daydreaming his "fantasy-cure" and compared its effectiveness to a visit to a spa or a hot spring.

Lichtenberg was the kind of procrastinator who does something remarkable when he is supposed to be doing something else. His scatteredness was the source of his genius. It was itself a seed.

For a while in the eighteenth century there was a pipeline between Germany and England that delivered the Continent's intellectuals to the island and in return sent some of England's minor lordlets back to the mainland for schooling. Well into the nineteenth century, it was said, a peculiar dialect of Hanoverian English was common in Göttingen, kind of a precursor to the global English that now radiates out from airports and Hyatts across most of the world.

Some of Lichtenberg's Göttingen students were young English aristocrats, and they were so impressed with their tutor that they arranged for Lichtenberg to visit England. George III, whose roots were in Hanover, took a liking to the professor, partly because they could speak German to each other, but also because Lichtenberg added a little academic gravitas to the court. Lichtenberg toured the observatory at Richmond with the king, and the two became so chummy that George III would drop by Lichtenberg's digs unannounced, seeking conversation with Herr Professor.

I decided to go to Göttingen to visit Lichtenberg's home and to learn what I could from the locals, but I worried a little about my almost complete ignorance of German. At one point before I left I had made tentative plans to take German lessons. When I say I made tentative plans, what I really mean is that for a while I told myself that I was going to find a German tutor, maybe some graduate student in need of funds, to teach me. But in fact I did nothing to actually find a German tutor. What I did instead was read a lot of articles online about the mental-health benefits of learning a second language. These articles led me to more, similar articles, including several about America's shameful lagging behind in language instruction, and finally an essay about America's historical antipathy for foreign languages. (Apparently, for a while in the 1920s, Nebraska had a law on the books that made the teaching of a foreign language illegal.) Reading all this made me want to reproach my fellow Americans—even though, of course, I was myself only reading these articles as a pretext for avoiding taking my own German lessons. The familiar postponer's dynamic was at work: the time I spent reading these articles about the need to learn another language excused me from the need to learn another language.

As a result of my failure to study German, during my brief time in Germany, I existed in a cocoon of incomprehension. On the train from Frankfurt to Göttingen, listening to a string of announcements in German, I understood nothing, and that lack of understanding fostered, with astonishing ease, a sense of paranoia. There was something about the German language—though I knew, of course, the fault was in me—that made me think I was constantly being yelled at, reprimanded. Every train-station announcement sounded like some sort of formal notification that I was about to be arrested for unspecified crimes.

I hoped that no one on the train would try to speak with me—not the conductor, not the ticket taker, not even the pretzel vendor. I didn't think I was ready for conversation. I spent most of the ride paging through my German-English/English-German phrasebook, studying how to say, just in case I would need to, "I am an American, where is the nearest toilet?"

Outside the train window was the history-haunted German countryside, dotted with actual castles in a few spots. The nostalgic view was disorienting, because the train was so much sleeker, cleaner, faster, and more futuristic than the commuter plodders back home, and yet the faster we sped, the further back in time we seemed to be racing, back to Henry the Proud, back to Otto the Great, back to forgotten, pusillanimous Carolingians, the past weirdly contiguous with the future.

Göttingen is ancient. To an American like me, a Midwesterner whose idea of really old architecture is the shopping mall left over from the mid-twentieth century, the city might as well be Troy. Göttingen avoided Allied bombing during World War II, and so one can still come across houses and halls erected in the 1300s. A piece of the medieval wall that once encircled the town is still standing along the Turmstrasse, and today it is a favorite place for local loiterers to drink beer and menace pedestrians. The great age of the place, in combination with an abundance of good-looking university students riding bikes everywhere, is appealing. At least I found it appealing. Lichtenberg, on the other hand, called Göttingen a "dreadful hole." But I suppose he earned the right to be so ungenerous because he made the place his home. Lichtenberg often talked of moving to Italy, home of his good friend Volta, but nothing ever came of it. Maybe he was daunted by his lack of Italian.

Lichtenberg was eventually rewarded for his loyalty to Göttingen with a number of local monuments erected in his honor. Next to the Paulinerkirche, which was the university library a half dozen centuries or so ago, a figure of Lichtenberg sits on a bench as if discoursing with his students, legs crossed like William F. Buckley Jr., his hump barely visible beneath the trailing ponytail of his wig. A few blocks away, behind the St.-Johannis-Kirche, he stands upright, all five feet of him, and his hump is pretty small here, too. Lichtenberg was such a little fellow that he is said to have sat on books while dining, so he could reach table height.

Göttingen loves its scientists, or at least it does now. In the 1930s, the Nazis decided the university there was a center of disreputable "Jewish physics"—fields like mathematical aerodynamics had pretty much been invented there—and nearly entire departments had to flee to the United States and United Kingdom. Today, many of the town's *strasses* are named for these persecuted thinkers, and plaques on some of the older buildings announce what intellectual once lived there.

One of the consequences of waiting as long as I did to make travel plans—that is, one of the costs of procrastination—is that by the time you get where you are going, you have no idea where you should eat or whom you should eat with. You forfeit the chance at advance planning. When I went alone to have dinner at an Italian restaurant next to my hotel, I took a seat in what I thought was the restaurant's bar area. It turned out to be an auxiliary all-purpose room used mostly by kitchen staff having a smoke on break. By the time I had figured out my mistake, I was too embarrassed to ask for another seat, maybe one in the actual dining room. Instead I decided to stick it out by myself in what I could now clearly see was *not* the bar area, where every so often a dishwasher would show up to have a smoke, look me over, and wonder why an American was eating in their break room. The friendliest face I saw all night belonged to a good-natured, short-legged mutt that walked in with one of the manager's friends. The dog had been left near me in the not-bar, while the manager and his friend chatted, and for a while I had a good time talking to the animal in a doggyish cartoon voice and sneaking him stray bits of antipasti. The kitchen staff seemed to know this mutt and they came out one at a time to pet him, play with him, and nuzzle him. I thought this was all pretty cute, until I remembered that this was the same kitchen staff that, as soon as they finished running their hands through this mutt's fur, would be preparing my next course. No problem, though. The dog could only have improved the food.

At no point during my visit did I manage to speak any German—partly due to my incompetence, and partly because most of the Germans I met spoke better English than I did. I remember spending a morning wandering the *Wochenmarkt* in the town square looking for conversation. I wanted to talk about Lichtenberg, but the locals I tried to speak with only wanted to ask me about David Foster Wallace or American politics, both bewildering topics in any language.

My social stumbles seemed apt. Lichtenberg claimed to be more comfortable watching humanity than interacting with it. Spying on the streetscape of Göttingen from his rooms, he would step back from the window when an acquaintance came into view, he said, to save them both the embarrassment of acknowledging each other. In England, Lichtenberg told William Herschel in a letter, he avoided tearooms and balls, and spent his time atop cathedral towers "with a field glass," at a remove from the passing scene, always spying.

Lichtenberg's watchfulness was of a piece with his procrastination, and so was his ambivalence. Coolness, emotional distance, a refusal to commit: all relieve us of the need to act. In Lichtenberg, there was both a Romantic inwardness and a scientific objectivity. He was both dreamer and empiricist. No wonder he sometimes didn't know what he was supposed to do.

Most of us are similarly compounded, dichotomous, conflicted: Tyger and Lamb, hero and schlub, Batman and Bruce Wayne. (A Roz Chast cartoon under the title "The Mind-Body Problem": A mope slumps on a couch. The mind, in a speech balloon, says, "Get up." The body says, "No.")

The multiple sides of our natures sometimes need to battle it out, and while the battle rages, there is nothing for us to do but postpone.

It makes sense that Lichtenberg is remembered so well in Göttingen, his hometown. Less predictably, he is also revered in Newnan, Georgia, a town about an hour south of Atlanta. Newnan is the world headquarters for the Lichtenbergian Society, a small fellowship of procrastinators who gather regularly to honor the group's namesake and his habitual dithering. Newnan is also home to the society's

founder, Dale Lyles, a retired teacher and community theater
director.

Dale lives in a handsome Craftsman bungalow on a
quiet side street just a few blocks from Newnan's courthouse
square, where instead of a figure of Lichtenberg, the requi-
site monumental Confederate soldier stands sentry. Behind
Dale's house is a backyard labyrinth he built a few years ago,
during a period when he was supposed to have been writing
an opera. Dale never did get around to writing the opera.
Instead, he devoted his energies to his backyard labyrinth
and to the adjacent fire pit and shade garden. Today it's a
pleasant, ferny place to spend a spring evening, cocktail in
hand. We'll get to the opera later.

It was in this very backyard that Lyles and his friends
formed the Lichtenbergian Society a few years ago. He
and a few of his friends from town had gathered for a party
marking the winter solstice, which seemed like as good
an excuse as any for celebration. They are an imaginative
bunch—composers, writers, artists, actors, a professional
clown. At that December gathering, during one of their
typically earnest, cocktail-fueled fireside discussions about
art and philosophy and literary criticism, someone quoted
one of Lichtenberg's aphorisms: "To do just the opposite is
also a form of imitation." Lyles had never heard of Lichtenberg, but he liked the sound of that aphorism. So he looked

Lichtenberg up on Wikipedia. He learned that Lichtenberg was an inspired dabbler, intellectually curious, ready to follow his curiosity from one discipline to another. Here was someone Lyles and his crowd could relate to. Then Lyles read this: "Lichtenberg was prone to procrastination."

Lyles and his friends, guys brimming with big ideas, but who only sometimes did anything about those ideas, knew about procrastination. It was their bane, and their secret pleasure. That night, Lyles came up with the idea of forming a society to honor Lichtenberg, the Enlightenment's paragon of delay. They worked out the details. The society would have elected officers and occasional meetings. There would be a charter. There would be cocktails.

Within a week (awfully expedient for a bunch of procrastinators) they had formed the Lichtenbergian Society and adopted a motto: *Cras melior est.*

Tomorrow is better.

For their first act, and remembering Lichtenberg's failure to write the *Tom Jones*-esque novel he had planned, each of the founding members of the society pledged to compose a few pages of his own bawdy, picaresque novel. But no more than a few pages. No one wanted to be too much of a go-getter about this.

Remarkably, the Lichtenbergians all made good on their pledge. Marc Honea, the society's newly elected aphorist, wrote a chapter that not only imitated Fielding's ornate Georgian prose, but also worked in lyrics from "It's Not Unusual" by the *other* Tom Jones, the Welsh pop star.

Of all the people I had met so far in my research, Dale Lyles was easily the most tolerant of procrastination. He was, in fact, just generally a really *nice guy*. The first time I called Dale Lyles on the phone, I interrupted him in the process of baking a batch of Corn Flake Crunchies for new neighbors who had just moved in. This act of kindness impressed me, but there was more forthcoming. Dale not only invited me down to Newnan for a chat, he also offered to gather the Lichtenbergians for a special meeting, solely for my benefit. This meeting happened in the shade and quiet of Lyles's backyard, where he had assembled an impressive portable bar and was tending a nice fire. The Lichtenbergians were welcoming hosts.

The society exists partly to encourage its members in their creative pursuits and partly to encourage them to procrastinate. Those two ends seem at first glance to be at odds with each other. But there is a certain Lichtenbergian logic at work, as well. Lyles's gorgeous backyard labyrinth was, for example, one product of the time Lyles spent not writing the opera he was supposed to be writing. Later, when he was supposed to be writing a score for a stage version of Nancy Willard's children's book *A Visit to William Blake's*

Inn, he instead wrote that opera he had been putting off earlier. Nothing much came of that opera. He entered it in a competition in Germany, which it did not win. But then again, Lyle says, when he finally did get around to writing the *William Blake's Inn* score, he did so with an increased confidence in his abilities as an orchestrator.

"The joke is that task avoidance is good because the world would be a better place if more artists would stop before inflicting their art on others," Lyles told me that night, as the Lichtenbergians and I sat by the fire. But here was evidence that task-avoidance could also be a kind of task-acceptance.

What I recall about that night were the prayer flags suspended around Dale's backyard and the chimes sounding. Dale had just made me a second bourbon-and-Tuaca cocktail. I was happy to sit back and listen to the Lichtenbergians talk about education and art and bad art and whether happiness is a worthy personal goal. The Lichtenbergian Society isn't just a bunch of slackers. It requires some level of effort from its members. According to the charter: "Members are expected, at some point prior to or following their addition to the rolls, to submit a creative work." But it also requires them to not get too overwrought about it. "In the spirit of the namesake of the SOCIETY, it is not required (or even, in fact, encouraged) that said work be either complete or successful."

For a Lichtenbergian, dawdling and delay and hesitation are all part of the creative process. Dale had noticed that to put off one thing often involved doing another. He had noticed that this second, unsanctioned thing often turned out to be a more worthy object of attention than the thing you were *supposed* to be doing. In this sense, it is possible, if you squint hard enough, to see procrastination as an active agent of accomplishment. Inspired, Dale began to write a book about this paradoxical idea.

That kind of initiative might earn him censure from the society.

Given that procrastination is a nearly universal habit, it is not surprising that every so often batches of procrastinators decide to form societies. And because procrastinators seem to have a fondness for tired jokes, you often see their gathering advertised along these lines: Procrastinator's Club Meeting—Postponed Until Tomorrow.

Some of these groups are modeled on support programs like Alcoholics Anonymous. They try to help procrastinators overcome the habit. Others celebrate delay unapologetically. An example of the second kind is the Procrastinators' Club of America, a Philadelphia-based organization founded in

1956 by Les Waas, an advertising executive. Waas, who died in 2016, made a career of writing commercial jingles, composing nearly a thousand of them, for clients that included Holiday Inn and the Ford Motor Company. The best known of these jingles remains the tune he wrote for Mister Softee ice-cream trucks. The company's trucks still play the song ("today's best-known ice-cream truck tune," says *The Oxford Handbook of Mobile Music Studies*, Vol. 2) as they cruise up and down summer streets in fifteen states.

Waas launched his Procrastinators' Club as a prank. At a Philadelphia hotel popular with reporters, he put up a sign announcing that the Procrastinators' Club meeting was delayed. The press demanded to know more about the club, so Waas felt obliged to found it. His official title was acting president. Waas never ascended to the full presidency, he liked to explain, because the committee tasked in 1957 with electing a standing club president had never gotten around to doing so.

Every so often, Waas organized field trips for the club's members. These excursions were almost always behind schedule. One excursion, in late 1965, went to the New York World's Fair. Unfortunately, the fair had closed eighteen months earlier. Later in the 1960s, Waas and his club organized antiwar protests. The specific conflict they objected to turned out to be the War of 1812. Waas considered the protests a success because, as he told a reporter, "The war is over now."

Waas's Procrastinators' Club and Lyles's Lichtenbergian Society are premised on the same jokey and willful subversion of conventional values: punctuality, efficiency, hustle. At annual meetings of the Lichtenbergian Society, members list their creative goals for the year ahead and review their progress on the previous year's goals. But if a member's work wins him *too much* recognition or too many other conventional measures of success, he is subject to censure.

Procrastination is, in one sense, a joke: you are supposed to do something and you don't; or you don't do what you are supposed to do when you are supposed to do it; or you do something other than the thing you are supposed to do. This is comedy. It's funny for the same reason that laughing at a funeral can be funny: because it's ridiculously inappropriate.

Procrastination is, on the other hand, also the most serious thing imaginable. We have only so much time to work with. Waste it and one day you will find yourself wondering where it all went. That's serious. It's so serious that you have to laugh about it to insulate yourself from the seriousness. You recognize that your life is a sequence of moments stacked end on end on one another until you run out of moments. You feel this reckoning weighing on you and know it must be confronted. But you are a procrastinator. The confrontation can wait.

There are so many ways to rationalize procrastination: it may be a defiant shot across the bow of an overbearing authority or a critique of the prevailing global-capitalist ethic. For writers like De Quincey and Oscar Wilde, procrastination was an element of personal style.

Writers may be the world's most persistent procrastinators, which is strange because they work in a trade in which the deadline is supposed to be sacrosanct. Author Douglas Adams said, "I love deadlines. I love the whooshing sound they make as they go by." When he died in 2001, he was twelve years past the deadline for his last book.

Writers are unmatched at excusing their own sluggishness. Does anyone talk about "accountant's block"? Does your auto mechanic claim to need a soulful, seaside stroll before getting down to work? Even pacing the floor, that cliché of the creative act, is a kind of postponement. I used to think that when I paced I was summoning big thoughts, getting my mental gears going by putting the physical in motion. But maybe all that ping-ponging back and forth was just a simulacrum of my psychic vacillation, my irresolution: Should I sit here or sit there? Write this or write that? Should I even be a writer at all? Maybe there is a way for me to make a living that doesn't require staring at blank paper and blinking cursors.

William Gass spent thirty years on his novel *The Tunnel*. Rilke had to work around the First World War and his own severe depressions to complete the *Duino Elegies* over the course of a decade. I'm not trying to directly compare myself to their likes. Rilke's topics were ontological torment and existential suffering. I have struggled with seven hundred words on cardigan sweaters for *GQ*. But Rilke knew that some work is done indirectly. "I have often asked myself whether those days on which we are forced to be indolent are not just the ones we pass in profoundest activity?" he wrote in a letter, presumably in lieu of doing actual work. "Whether all our doing, when it comes later, is not only the last reverberation of a great movement which takes place in us on those days of inaction."

This is exactly the kind of magical thinking every pro-crastinator must master. Inaction isn't really inaction, but an unseen stirring that leads only later to some useful result. Yes, I suppose I could spend the day in dutiful work, doing what I'm supposed to be doing. But if I instead clean out the pencil drawer—who knows what wonders may result? Can I really afford to spend my day doing mere work?

Some procrastinators blame their habit on perfectionism or fear of failure. The idea is that they can't do anything until they know they'll do it just right. Many of us are stalled by the knowledge of our own insufficiency. Mr. Casaubon, the pedant classicist in George Eliot's *Middlemarch*, can't bring himself to cease his laborious preliminary research and launch into the actual writing of his masterwork. Given his working title, "Key to All Mythologies," readers can only be grateful for his hesitation.

Casaubon is a ridiculous character, which may be another way of saying he stands in for many of us. His habitual avoidance—at once self-protective and self-frustrating—is something most procrastinators would understand. His creator must have understood, too. Eliot has been held up as a heroine of the dilatory artist. She didn't start writing fiction until her mid-thirties, and had to be nudged ahead by friends, even then.

But in the literature of indecision, no one has dithered as profoundly as Hamlet, the student prince and ancestor to today's procrastinating undergraduates. (Is it not fitting that Hamlet's delay has been the subject of so many English papers written at the last possible minute?) If the old honor code of familial revenge had been good enough for Hamlet, his response to his father's death would have been automatic. But Hamlet was a new kind of existential hero, which means that before he can do his job—killing the king, in his case—he has to agonize over who he is, what he is here for, the meaning of life, the mysteries of eternity. All of this is inconvenient, but it is what makes him one of us. He is undone by his own free will, by his choices, by his impulsiveness.

Researchers say that procrastination is just a variety of impulsiveness, a failure to regulate urges and desires. If this is true, Hamlet's delay is just the flip side of the rashness he displays in killing Polonius. On the other hand: Hamlet's procrastination has been analyzed and debated for centuries, but does it really need to be explained at all? After all, it's not all that strange that he hesitates to kill his uncle. What would be strange and disturbing is if he raced to take a life without compunction. For Hamlet, acting—both in the sense of play-acting and in the sense of resolving to move on a difficult decision—is suspect. To act is to play, to pretend. Action is, in this sense, inauthentic. Inaction and procrastination are more likely to contain truth. The martial honor code that vexes Hamlet has no use for ambivalence or conscience or introspection. Like Taylorism, it is absolute in its insistence on "one best way."

I got my start as a procrastinator the way most of us did, by putting off all the chores—cleaning my room, weeding the garden, taking out the trash—assigned to me as a kid. A child who puts off his chores isn't just putting off his chores. He is also prolonging his childhood, staving off the responsible life. On Saturday mornings, when I should have been making my bed, I was watching television cartoons. There was Wile E. Coyote eternally pursuing the Road Runner. Even then I sensed that there was something heartbreaking about the idea of a pursuit that never quite ends, a dream never quite realized, an undertaking that can never be completed. There was something heroic about Wile E. Coyote. I also understood that there was something stupid about Wile E. Coyote. You can't deny the stupidity of a creature who continually blows himself up by lighting a match so he can see in the darkness of a dynamite shed. But the fact of his stupidity didn't negate his heroism—not even when he stands directly under the falling rock he himself had managed to dislodge from a steep cliff.

Saturday-morning cartoons were my first encounter with the romance of process. To be on the verge of something is to be endlessly becoming. Possibility never exhausted. I guess this is what makes Wile E. Coyote a romantic hero, in addition to a complete idiot. The beginning of any process may be the most daunting time, but it is also the most hopeful. It's when we can feel limitless potential. Writers are paralyzed by the prospect of writing something lousy. They fear failing. The good news is that as long as a work remains in formation it might turn out to be brilliant. (Anything is possible.)

This is one reason that procrastinators don't like to complete their projects. As long as they are still working on them, they can still aspire to perfection. As soon as you finish a project, it becomes just another well-meaning (but failed) effort by another imperfect creator. The early Gnostic teacher Basilides thought that being itself was a form of degradation; only nonexistence could claim perfection. To bring something into existence, then, is to ruin it. (This may explain why the inspired idea that comes to me on my walk home from the subway usually turns out, when I write it down upon arriving home, to be not very inspired at all.)

So the procrastinator wants to prolong process. He wants to postpone his story's climax, because his real aim isn't to reach his goal but to continue to seek it. The realization of something long dreamed of only depletes the possibilities, caps the limits.

As long as the process continues, anything can happen. The romance of process gestures toward the eternal. The lovers in Keats's "Ode on a Grecian Urn" remain forever and always about to kiss. This is the ultimate deferral, the romance of process frozen in the timelessness of art. "Though winning near the goal yet, do not grieve," the poet tells the lovers. There is no end to their becoming.

On the evening of my visit to Newnan, Georgia, I shared with Dale Lyles my ideas about process and delay and the Grecian urn. It helped that I'd had a few drinks at dinner. Dale had taken me to a burger place called Meat 'N Greet, where I drank, if I'm remembering this correctly, one of their specialty cocktails, the Stinko de Mayo. Later, we walked through the center of Newnan and stopped to check out the monument of the Confederate soldier in the courthouse square and a plaque memorializing the Battle of Brown's Mill, fought in 1864 just outside Newnan. The battle was the result of a Union raid that sought, among other things, to seize nearby Andersonville Prison and liberate the thirty thousand or so federal troops held prisoner in bestial conditions there. But the raid was bungled, the Union effort frustrated, and the Rebels won the day at Brown's Mill. The result was another thirteen hundred Union prisoners added to the rolls at Andersonville.

Andersonville is famously cited in etymologies of the word "deadline." The word originally referred to a marked perimeter past which no prisoner could venture without risk of being shot. Today the term means something different, but is no less fraught, for procrastinators. The American Civil War also produced one of history's great procrastinators, the Union general and infamous foot-dragger George McClellan. At the head of Union forces for a little less than a year, McClellan demonstrated an almost religious devotion to preparation and planning. He planned and prepared so much, in fact, that he often never got around to doing the things for which he was preparing and planning. He was reluctant to take the fight to the enemy. This got under the skin of his colleagues. His fellow general Henry Halleck fumed in high style, "There is an immobility here that exceeds all that any man can conceive of. It requires the lever of Archimedes to move this inert mass." President Lincoln was characteristically pithier. He said McClellan had a case of "the slows."

The problem wasn't that McClellan's army did nothing. The problem was that they did everything but what Lincoln wanted, which was to attack the enemy. Always there was another reconnaissance to be made, more training to be done, more parades to be had. McClellan, like a lot of great generals, was a perfectionist and a control freak. But in his case, perfectionism seems to have masked an insecurity, an interior doubt about his own abilities. The result was endless tinkering, adjusting, reconsidering, and starting over.

His meticulous preparation was the military equivalent of a school kid sharpening pencils to avoid writing a book report.

It occurred to me during my time in Georgia, among all the monuments to Confederate soldiery, that my obsession with procrastination had made everything about the Civil War seem bizarrely, anachronistically psychological: a decision deferred (I'm thinking here of the American Ur-question about what to do about slavery, the one question the Founders couldn't quite bring themselves to grapple with); an ambivalent body politic, torn schizophrenically in two; self-destructive impulsivity loosed, tragically, on a national scale. The war could be considered a lesson in the costs of procrastination, in which the failure to deal with a problem promptly produces even greater troubles, for an entire republic.

Dale and I, as we walked around the Newnan town square, were talking about the procrastinator's ability to rationalize his or her habit. McClellan wouldn't have recognized himself as a procrastinator. He would have seen himself as *thorough*. And, to be fair, an excess of caution and preparation may be understandable in a person responsible for the lives of tens of thousands of soldiers. McClellan fiercely defended himself and his battlefield dithering all his life, even running for president against his old boss, Lincoln, in 1864. But in fact McClellan was an example of the kind of self-protective procrastinator who finds refuge in the belief that he will be better equipped to handle any particular challenge at some point in the future. That is to say, he was, at least in his own mind, not a procrastinator at all.

Lichtenberg, on the other hand, never commanded anything but a lecture hall audience. He could afford to be slack. But he also expressed anguish at the opportunities he let pass. Lichtenberg, too, was thorough. He was always planning something big that never quite materialized—like the big picaresque novel in which he was going to "use everything." So Lichtenberg went in every direction at once, following the trail of his curiosity wherever it led him. The results could be chaotic and confused (see his notebooks) but also luminous (see his notebooks).

Lichtenberg recognized that his approach was idiosyncratic, and also that, by the conventional scientific standards of the day, it had failed. This is how, late in his life, he summarized his career: "I have covered the way to science like dogs which go for a walk with their masters, backward and forward a hundred times over, and when I arrived I was tired."

But even this admission of defeat, in its self-effacing charm, is evidence of Lichtenberg's victory. Dale Lyles and his friends found in him just what so many others have found—a wit, a skepticism, an elegance of expression that cannot be separated from his habit for delay.

"I had to find out who this Lichtenberg fellow was," Dale told me when I asked him about starting his society.

This, then, must be another reason that the procrastinator postpones. We postpone because we understand that our deferral will somehow connect us to others similarly disposed. In this way, our *no* will function as a *yes*.

I had thought that by flying off to Germany, and later by going to visit Dale Lyles in Georgia, I was cleverly ducking the real work waiting to be done. But already on the flight home from Atlanta, I was making plans for another trip. And from my lofty perspective in seat 11D, Delta flight 2350, a perch higher than the one Lichtenberg never ascended to in the balloon he never launched, it occurred to me that I wasn't even procrastinating correctly. I was checking off my diversionary travels like some kind of go-getter. In the process of trying to avoid one task, I was in fact completing many other tasks. Even procrastinators can become task-oriented, when the task they are oriented to is procrastinating.

7

‖‖‖

THEREFORE BIND ME

*Therefore, take me and bind me to the crosspiece halfway up
the mast; bind me as I stand upright with a bond so fast that
I cannot possibly break away and lash the rope ends to the
mast itself. If I beg and pray you to set me free, then bind me
more tightly still.*
—HOMER, *THE ODYSSEY*, BOOK XII, TRANSLATED BY
SAMUEL BUTLER

All roads, for me at least, seemed to lead to procrastination,
a cliché that became literal truth one day when I got lost
driving through western Pennsylvania.

I was in Pennsylvania looking for Fallingwater, the

weekend home Frank Lloyd Wright had designed for a department store magnate named Edgar Kaufmann in the wilds south of Pittsburgh. Fallingwater is one of those structures that inspires reverence in a certain kind of architecture buff. I have never been that kind of architecture buff. Still, I understood the urge to make a pilgrimage there, at least once. Going to Fallingwater is like a pilgrimage in that the place is in the middle of nowhere and getting there takes, if not a spiritual commitment, then at least a willingness to navigate rural roads in a region where the hills render GPS impotent. In this craggy country, you see a lot of front-yard replicas—I *assume* they're replicas—of the Ten Commandments, stone tablets serving as lawn ornaments.

Fallingwater is set in a basin of sandstone and rhododendron on the slope of Laurel Ridge, one of the westernmost wrinkles in the series of mountains that delayed American westward expansion during the colonial era. Driving these hills and valleys on my way to Fallingwater, I could understand how impassable the trackless wilderness must have seemed to, say, an eighteenth-century farmer trying to deliver goods to markets. Something about these hollows and striations was disorienting. And it must not have helped that I was absentmindedly musing on eighteenth-century produce transport as I drove, because I got myself deeply, deeply lost.

Procrastination, I thought to myself as I drove in circles, is a kind of lost-ness. It is a temporal disorientation, whereas at that moment I was experiencing a geospatial disorientation. I was really lost. The difference, I guess, is that the procrastinator chooses disorientation. Procrastination is really a kind of time travel, then, an attempt to manipulate time by transferring activities from the concrete present to an abstract future. My own procrastination tour was both time travel and plain old geographical travel, though my temporal disorientation was at the moment nothing compared to my geospatial disorientation. I had no idea where I was.

It was only when I stopped at a Pizza Hut for directions (the exotic dance club/tanning parlor was closed) that I saw how close I was, not only to Fallingwater, but also to old Fort Necessity. This colonial-era stockade, a much cruder structure than the house Wright would design twelve miles away and almost two hundred years later, is important in its own way. It was near Fort Necessity that British and French soldiers in 1754 fought the first battle of the global conflict that would be called the Seven Years' War. The immediate provocation for this conflict, according to my high school history textbook, had been provided by twenty-two-year-old Lieutenant Colonel George Washington of the militia of the province of Virginia, who had been sent earlier that year by Virginia's British governor to chase French forces off the site of what is now Pittsburgh, at the head of the Ohio River. Both the French and the British understood—as I began to understand during my search for Fallingwater—how difficult this mountainous country was to traverse, and so they wanted to control the river corridors that allowed for more rapid transport through the interior. On their way to Pittsburgh, to secure the riverside site for the British and their colonies, Washington's forces ambushed a French detachment and killed its commander and thirteen soldiers. Or, as the French saw it, murdered them. War on.

Washington pretty much bungled that operation. His reputation as a military commander is based instead on his management of the Continental Army, later, in the Revolutionary War. And one of Washington's greatest successes in *that* war came about partly due to the procrastination of his opponent. Twelve years after ambushing the French in western Pennsylvania, Washington launched another, more successful surprise attack, on Christmas night in New Jersey. This time he was fighting in the service of the newly independent United States, and again it wasn't going well. His army was battered, nearly ruined. Needing a victory to survive, Washington gambled everything on a coup de main, beginning with a moonlight crossing of the Delaware River in small boats. Somehow, it worked. The subsequent rout of Hessian troops in Trenton revived Patriot hopes and secured the general's place among history's great military leaders. Washington's victory was made easier by the incompetence of the Hessian commander Johann Rall. The story is that Rall, during a Christmas evening game of cards, had been handed a note detailing the approach of Washington's troops, as witnessed by local loyalists. Rall, not wanting to be interrupted mid-game, pocketed the note unread, intending to get to it later.

Now that I had started looking for it, I could find procrastination everywhere, even in textbook American history.

Back to Fallingwater. It is said that for years guides at Fallingwater told visitors that the land on which the house was built had once been owned by Washington. No evidence supports that claim, though. Kaufmann bought the property in 1916 and built a summer camp for his department store employees there, which operated into the 1930s. In a photo from the 1920s, you can see employees in one-piece swimsuits bathing under the waterfall at Bear Run. The fall, the rocks, the riverbed are all recognizable as the same over which Wright's house now seems to hover, the same land Washington may have once trod.

I had come looking for Fallingwater (once the good people at Pizza Hut set me on the right path) because Wright was another of the history-making achievers who are sometimes identified as great procrastinators. Wright's status as dawdler is based on the legend behind his work on Fallingwater. The story of Wright's delay at Fallingwater has been told and retold so many times that it seems it must be apocryphal. It sounds too good to really be true. Asked by Kaufmann to build a retreat for him and his family along a cascading section of Bear Run, Wright agreed. He then spent the next nine months doing no visible work on the design. This inactivity continued until Kaufmann, the story goes, one day surprised Wright by announcing he would be dropping by his studio to look at the long-promised but never-produced drawings for the house. His bluff called, Wright had to haul ass. A Wright apprentice named Edgar Tafel later wrote in his *Years With Frank Lloyd Wright*, that Wright, hearing that his client was waiting, "briskly emerged from his office . . . sat down at the table set with the plot plan and started to draw . . . The design just poured out of him. 'Liliane and E.J. will have tea on the balcony . . . they'll cross the bridge to walk in the woods . . .' Pencils being used up as fast as we could sharpen them . . . Erasures, overdrawing, modifying. Flipping sheets back and forth. Then, the bold title across the bottom 'Fallingwater.' A house has to have a name." Taffel's account suggests that the entire process took maybe two hours.

I don't know if that's a reasonable or even plausible amount of time to produce a design that would stand at the peak of American architectural history, but that's the official story. It raises the question: Why didn't Wright just get to work when he was supposed to?

It wasn't as if Wright could afford to coast. At the time Kaufmann commissioned his weekend home, Wright had descended into obscurity. Though Wright had come to prominence earlier in the century, he was now pretty much a has-been. Critics derided him. A landmark 1932 architecture show at the Museum of Modern Art had mostly ignored Wright in favor of a new wave of European modernists, including Mies van der Rohe and Gropius and Le Corbusier. Taliesin, Wright's home and workshop in southwest Wisconsin, was on the cusp of foreclosure. The Depression had severely limited the number of new commissions available to residential architects; not so many people were building fancy new homes. For Wright, then, Fallingwater should have been an opportunity to be seized, a chance for a heroic comeback. The only way to explain the nine months Wright spent *not* working on Fallingwater is by procrastination's perverse logic. Nothing was about the only thing that could be done in such a situation.

For all its modernity, for all its of-the-moment Cubist showing-off, Wright's design for Fallingwater may be most remarkable for the way it makes a bid for timelessness. Kaufmann, the story goes, had expected Wright to design him a weekend home on the banks of Bear Run, but slightly downstream from those falls. He expected to get a place that would give him a view of the falls. Wright, instead, sited the house *on* the falls, seemingly floating over the falls. The house wrapped itself around bedrock and water, as if wanting to make itself an element of the eternal landscape. The house, in fact, absorbs the landscape, and this creates an aura of permanence, of belonging to the land, that no built work can really aspire to. Buildings eventually fall. Fallingwater itself came so close to collapse in the 1990s that structural engineers had to be called in to shore it up. So much for permanence.

I had been wanting to go to Fallingwater for so long, had been planning it for so long, that once I got there I hardly knew where to look or what to do. I don't mean that the house was in any way a disappointment. It's just that I felt some need to make more of the experience than it actually was. I had seen so many pictures of it that encountering the house itself seemed a little counterfeit. The house seemed an inadequate reproduction of the beautiful photos I had seen in so many architecture books.

It wasn't just me. The tour guide had gathered ten or so of us to walk the grounds together and I noticed we all did pretty much the same thing: we stared at the house, hard, almost leaning forward to extract every last bit of significance out of what we were seeing. I would have been embarrassed to say anything as simple or as honest as "This is really beautiful."

Architecture does this to people. It is like wine in that way. It encourages a lot of know-it-all posturing and declamation. From men, especially. On our house tour, a retired physician from Virginia went on at some length about his belief that Wright used cork for the walls of one of the bathrooms. A vacationing history teacher couldn't stop talking about the light.

Wright himself encouraged this sort of behavior, with his own over-the-top alpha-male salesmanship. Fallingwater was never just a house. It was instead "a great blessing—one of the great blessings to be experienced here on earth." To Kaufmann, he wrote "I conceived a love of you quite beyond the ordinary relationship of client and Architect. That love gave you Fallingwater. You will never have anything more in your life like it." Wright was always sending off notes like this. I especially love that he felt the need to capitalize "Architect" but not "client."

It's this nearly religious orientation to architecture that

makes visiting a Wright site feel like a pilgrimage. You feel as though you are not so much admiring a beautifully designed home as partaking in a sacrament. And then there's the simple fact of the remoteness of so many Wright buildings. I drove six hours to get to Fallingwater, which is about as close to a pilgrim's journey as I'll ever get. And I'd have to make a similar effort to get to Taliesin, his house in rural southwestern Wisconsin, or his Dana-Thomas House in Springfield, Illinois, or his Price Tower in Bartlesville, Oklahoma. More than any other great architect, Wright made his mark as much in the provinces as in the big cities. Maybe this distance from the usual cultural capitals lends Wright's most remote buildings a kind of standoffish power. With Fallingwater, Wright talked about besting the European modernists who had surpassed him in prominence. All the more remarkable that he did so in the backwoods of western Pennsylvania. The setting belies Wright's ambitions and pretensions, his gestures toward the spiritual. After all, one of the last things you pass before turning off the road approaching Fallingwater is an enormous statue of Yogi Bear welcoming RVs into his neighboring Jellystone Park.

Pilgrimage is a procrastinator's business in the sense that the pilgrim is undertaking a once-in-a-lifetime trek, one imbued with spiritual import. Pilgrimage by definition can't be done right away, or on an impulse. That's not a pilgrimage, that's a whim. Also, it helps to delay pilgrimage to allow the passage of time to accrue in credit to the object of the pilgrimage. The longer the site has waited for the pilgrim, the deeper the devotion. The older the relic, the better. This is why procrastinators make the best pilgrims.

In my chain hotel off the Pennsylvania Turnpike, the morning after my visit to Fallingwater, I was standing in line for my complimentary coffee and stale raisin bread in the breakfast room off the lobby when a man took a place in line next to me and asked, "How was your journey?"

I was barely awake, had not really counted on having to converse with anyone, and wasn't at all sure what this man was talking about. Did he mean my journey to Fallingwater? But he couldn't have known that I had been there. Or did he mean my morning's journey down from my room to the line for coffee and stale raisin bread? That didn't seem any more likely. He couldn't possibly have been referring to any kind of metaphorical journey, could he? Was he asking me how my search for understanding was progressing?

Confused, I decided to bluff my way through.

I said, "Good. It was a good journey. How was yours?"

And the man said, "I'm just glad to be here. It's a gift to

be here and we have to make the most of every day. I believe that sincerely."

Now I really had no idea what was happening. I had the feeling, though, that I was about to be asked to join some kind of church, so I grabbed my piece of stale raisin bread and wished the man a good day. Just to be sure, I took my food back to my room.

What had so unsettled me? Had the man said anything wrong? Could I find any holes in his philosophy? Had I been a little rude?

I had come to Fallingwater looking for evidence of Wright's procrastination, but what I found, inevitably, was evidence of my own. I knew I was there as an excuse, to buy time, because I was not yet ready to sit down and write. So in that sense, my journey was a difficult, even lousy one. Because who wants to drive the width of Pennsylvania just to find out how far he will go to avoid the work he should be doing? Here I was eating stale raisin bread on a king-size bed in a Hampton Inn watching *SportsCenter* with the sound down when I might have been accomplishing something. No wonder I had run from the man I met in line for my stale raisin bread. He and his hotel-lobby philosophy of gratitude put me to shame.

Wright had his own talent for self-sabotage, which is probably the signal characteristic of any procrastinator. In

1909, having just designed Robie House and Unity Temple, two of his greatest triumphs, he ran off to Europe with the wife of one of his clients. On the verge of the greatness he had worked so tirelessly for, what else was there to do but derail his own ascendant career?

It is possible that in those nine months before Kaufmann's surprise visit, Wright might have experienced some kind of creative paralysis brought on by the gravity and urgency of the project facing him—he might have choked, like a relief pitcher brought in with the bases loaded who can't seem to find the strike zone. He might have procrastinated out of fear that he really wasn't up to the job. Or he might have procrastinated out of despair at the tatters of his finances and his art-historical reputation. Or maybe there were more and more times when he just couldn't manage to give a damn about his work. He had tried to civilize the rich bastards. He had tried to bring a little soul to the tawdry carnival of American culture. He had built Robie House and Unity Temple and so much else, and where had any of it got him? The bastards were endlessly complaining about the structural flaws in the buildings he'd made for them. When one called to say that the ceiling Wright designed was leaking on his head during a dinner party, Wright told him to move his chair.

Or, as with Leonardo, Wright may not have been such

a chronic procrastinator after all. The architectural scholar Franklin Toker, in his book *Fallingwater Rising*, argues that even if Wright had waited until the last minute to commit his plans for the house to paper, his ideas must have been percolating all the while. He must have had the designs in his head. This is something like what I tell my wife when she finds me snoozing on the couch: I may look like I'm taking a nap, but I'm really writing. I'm always writing.

Wright was certainly an unrivaled self-promoter and his acolytes were always ready to help spread his legend. So it's revealing that Wright's apprentices didn't hesitate to spread the story of his waiting until the last minute to commit the Fallingwater designs to paper. After all, that delay might seem to suggest that the master was irresponsible or even lazy and had to be goaded into work by his hectoring clients. But Wright's students knew how people like to romanticize the creative process. In daily practice, procrastination can be boring and frustrating, but for a great artist, the habit can be pictured as a kind of muse, just the way madness sometimes is. Procrastinators, like the mad, are wild, rule-breaking, boundary-shattering. What Wright's apostles—and most of us—find appealing about the Fallingwater legend is that it confirms what we need to have confirmed—that there are people in the world to whom the usual conventions of art and commerce do not apply. Wright, his apprentices would have us know, was one such genius. He was a person who, given a problem to solve, would make his way through the world for some period of time, apparently doing nothing of consequence, but really the entire time *creating*. And then, as if by magic, at the very moment of crisis, such a person might simply translate his mental conceptions to paper and then, eventually, to stone and steel and glass, all perched over a waterfall in western Pennsylvania.

Most procrastinators don't experience their habit as heroic. We are frustrated—*panicked!!!*—by our inability to get anything done. A siege mentality sets in. The novelist Jonathan Franzen told a reporter from the *New York Times* that he wrote large portions of his best-selling novel *The Corrections* while wearing a blindfold, earplugs, and earmuffs to block out distractions. He wanted to eliminate the temptation to do anything other than write. For Franzen, those temptations included naps, card games, and "idle fiddling with power tools."

Franzen's account raises some troubling questions. For starters: Is it really possible that an American male of Franzen's generation would own *earmuffs?* But also: Are we now more distracted than people ever have been? That has been the consensus, with distraction cast as the enemy to be defeated by centeredness and mindfulness and the laser-like focus of the time budget. The virtual-world distractions that tempt us at work—tweeting, online gambling, fantasy sports, online shopping, porn, Pinterest, clips from last night's *Conan*—have inspired a neologism: cyberloafing. It is a bit of jargon as redolent of our age as "scientific shoveling" was of Taylor's.

The drive to eliminate such distractions has produced a small industry of software, surveillance technologies, and apps with names like Concentrate! and Think. There is money to be made in protecting ourselves from our impulses. Among the acknowledgments for her novel *NW*, Zadie Smith thanked the Internet-blocking apps Freedom and SelfControl for helping to free her from distraction.

The war on distraction predates the Internet, of course. If you have ever killed an afternoon at work biting at clickbait, following one dubious link after another, you probably have come across the story of Hugo Gernsback and his Isolator. Gernsback's story shows up on a lot of "weird news" sites—just the sort of destination that exists mainly to give us something else to do besides whatever it is we're supposed to be doing. A writer, editor, and slick businessman, Gernsback launched the magazine *Amazing Stories* in 1926 and is sometimes called the Father of Science Fiction, although he preferred to call his genre Scientifiction. Between 1913 and 1929, he also edited a magazine called *Science and Invention*, a forum for tinkerers and amateur experimenters. Procrastinators share Gernsback's fascination with the future. We believe the future is the best time to do anything we are supposed to be doing now.

It was in the July 1925 edition of this magazine that he introduced his Isolator, a device to help writers and other mental laborers focus on the task at hand. The Isolator reduces distractions by encasing the user in a helmet something like a deep-sea diver's, tethered by a hose to an oxygen tank. The helmet shelters the user from outside noise and reduces his field of vision to whatever can be seen through a narrow slit: that is, about one line of text.

A photo from the magazine shows Gernsback scribbling away in the quietude of the Isolator. At least the photo is said to be of Gernsback; it's impossible to say who's beneath the helmet. Whoever it is looks like he has been outfitted for a moon landing, so it is all the more comical that he is doing nothing more adventurous than scribbling away at an office desk.

Gernsback collected eighty patents for his various inventions, including an electric comb and hairbrush and a device that made it possible to use one's teeth for hearing. A self-promoter who liked to use a monocle to peruse restaurant menus, Gernsback won some limited fame as a crackpot tinkerer in the American tradition. In 1963 *Life* magazine called him a "Barnum for the Space Age." He never patented the Isolator, but his idea anticipated Franzen in his earmuffs and blindfold.

⸻

Gernsback in his hazmat-suit-like Isolator, Franzen in his earmuffs: these are images of individuals seeking shelter, as if fending off assault. This is a stance relative to the world that suggests fear and anxiety—and so, is it really a surprise to find it so often in writers?

It was once possible to think of writers as a special category of procrastinator, in the sense that their workdays and their relationships to editors were different from the relationship of a more conventionally employed person to the boss in the corner office. Putting off work on a long overdue draft of a novel seemed different from waiting until the last minute to write up an agenda for the weekly staff meeting. But the rise of the contract workforce has changed all that. Now entire sections of Brooklyn and Chicago and Portland and Austin are populated almost entirely by loitering freelancers—which is to say procrastinators. When you are free to set your own schedule, you are also free to disregard it completely. When you can work for years without ever meeting your employer, deadline discipline may be hard to maintain. The blithe dereliction characteristic of our contract economy has helped normalize procrastination.

Yet reading procrastination simply as a symptom of our distracted age seems neither historically nor philosophically accurate. First of all, people have been procrastinating—and hating themselves for it—for centuries. The habit predates not only the Internet but the steam locomotive, the toaster, whatever. So, yes, the Twitter feed may be surging, and the Netflix queue bulging. But procrastinators still have agency. They have options—maybe too many options. The Internet blocker Freedom is so named even though (or exactly because) its purpose is to constrain, to reduce options. Likewise, users of SelfControl are really subcontracting the job of controlling themselves. They have washed their hands of the job. And isn't it bizarre that when we want to protect ourselves from distraction, we depend on the very devices we find so distracting?

Distractions are really just choices. Choosing, though, is a bitch. We want more than one thing, but can have only one thing. We want freedom, but freedom scares the crap out of us. We don't know ourselves and therefore don't really know what we want. One self wants one thing; another, something else. One of the most basic splits is between my self at this moment and my self of the future. My self at this moment may want to blow off my obligations; my self of the future will have to reckon with the consequences. Procrastination happens when we have trouble reconciling the competing factions within the parliament of our selves.

When the war between the selves gets really intense, some self-restraint might be called for. This is why Odysseus, the hero of Greek legend, is name-dropped in so many discussions of distraction and self-control. You remember the story: Needing to resist the song of the Sirens, the dangerous enchantresses whose music lured sailors to their deaths on a rocky coast, Odysseus ordered his crew to bind him to the mast of his ship as they approached the Sirens' home. He restrained himself from temptation before temptation struck, and his forethought saved him. (What is too often overlooked about the old story is that the self-binding wasn't Odysseus's idea. It was suggested to him by Circe, an accomplished temptress herself and thus presumably an authority on how to avoid temptation.) Gernsback's Isolator suit is one bizarre example of self-binding, directly descended from Odysseus. So is the drug Antabuse, which produces very unpleasant side effects in combination with alcohol, and which some in recovery use to avoid the temptation to drink. It is made by Odyssey Pharmaceuticals.

It is difficult for me to think about these old Greek

stories as anything but tales of rampant procrastination. How else can you explain Odysseus's tortuous route home after the war, his restless wandering around the Mediterranean world, but as an effort to put off domestication? And his wife, Penelope, is an even more accomplished procrastinator. Back in Ithaca, waiting for her husband's return, she was besieged by a mob of 108 suitors, each sure that Odysseus was long since dead and each wishing to take his place. (Doesn't the number recall Albert Ellis's 100 requests for a date?) Who could blame her if Penelope had had her own doubts about her husband? But her excuse for staving off her suitors was brilliant. She claimed to be weaving a burial shroud for her elderly father-in-law and insisted that there could be no wooing until she completed the job. For three years she weaved the robe, and each night undid the previous day's work, thus extending the project indefinitely. Her trick has become part of the lore of marital fidelity, but for me it makes her the foremost heroine of procrastination. She demonstrated how delay, cunning, and deception (even self-deception) can be heroic.

Every year I put off getting a flu shot. Since I would prefer not to come down with the flu, this makes no sense. The problem is that shots are unpleasant and doctors' offices are even more unpleasant, so things get complicated. Getting a flu shot should be a simple thing, but any procrastinator who thinks about it long enough can make it a very complicated thing. A dilemma. Why do I put off my flu shot? Partly it's a matter of language. It's called a shot, and so it inspires fear. It becomes something to be dodged. This is one of the skills any procrastinator picks up—the ability to postpone an action by dithering, which dithering itself often produces rationalizations (however flimsy) to justify further inaction.

This is sometimes called overthinking, but that's too self-congratulatory, if you ask me. It makes it sound as if the procrastinator's problem is really his unstoppable mental prowess, which cannot be harnessed and so runs away with itself. Dithering is just a rerouting of one's thinking, away from action and toward inaction. Spend enough time *thinking* about things and you may not have to *do* any of them. All health care can be seen as a form of procrastination, I tell myself. Its object is to postpone a perfectly natural process—in this case, death. Maybe the people lined up for flu shots are the real procrastinators.

Healing is itself paradoxical. Doctors cut into us, they drug us, they invade our bodies, all in the name of health. We submit to regimens of pain and violence for the sake of long life. To be a patient is to be impatient—not just with the hours in the reception rooms, not just with the wait for test results, but with the loss of control of our own lives that we all experience as part of being doctored. Are we ever more aware of our own bodies than we are while sitting in a doctor's waiting room? Even the most routine checkup is disorienting, a break in the regulating logic of daily life. My competencies and facilities, my assets and education mean nothing once the doctor tells me to strip. Even before illness disarms us, the routines of health care expose us as vulnerable. *How do I tie this paper robe? Where do I look when the doctor's hands start to probe?*

Illness, too, is a postponement, an interim state. It is a recess from the everyday, something every schoolkid who has ever faked the flu to avoid an exam knows. This deception was something I never had much success with as a kid, which maybe in retrospect helps explain my adult tendency to procrastinate. Am I still trying to call a halt to the proceedings, to defy the governing schedule of my life? Healthy kids will feign coughs and sore throats not just because they're unready for the spelling test, but because they're attracted to the disorientation and novelty of illness. They find in illness a gratifying release from the mundane. Sitting on a couch at home watching TV and playing video games may be nothing special in itself, but as a break from the daily schedule of homeroom, science, and study hall it's delicious. Kids romanticize illness in exactly the way Susan Sontag warned against in *Illness as Metaphor*. Illness makes you interesting.

Tuberculosis was once so strongly associated with creativity that when medicine began to control the disease, critics feared for the impact on literature. Sontag quotes Byron admiring his own pallor and wishing to die of consumption: "Because the ladies would all say, 'Look at that poor Byron, how interesting he looks in dying.'"

The kid home sick from school senses his specialness, too. Who can blame him? Illness—even a bogus cold—transforms you. When you stay home from school, you become a presence in the classroom in a way that you never could be if you were actually there. People worry about you. Your friends deliver your homework to you at home.

One of the clichés of biography is the catastrophic injury or illness that changes or in retrospect explains a life. Theodore Roosevelt's youthful asthma, Franklin Roosevelt's polio, Beethoven's deafness, St. Ignatius's encounter with a cannonball at the Battle of Pamplona. Before Jack Kerouac became famous as the official novelist of the Beat generation, he was a speedy fullback for his high-school football team in Lowell, Massachusetts. A sports-crazy kid, he dreamed of starring in the Rose Bowl or winning the world heavyweight title. He settled for a spot on the freshman team at Columbia University. In his first game, against St. Benedict's Prep of New Jersey, he broke his leg returning a punt. His coaches had doubts about the severity of Kerouac's injury and accused him of "malingering." I picture the incipient hipster lounging around the locker room with his pipe, admonishing the jocks that their sweaty efforts were a waste of karmic energy. "Scrimmage, my ass," he wrote in the voice of his alter ego, Jack Duluoz, in the novel *Visions of Cody*. "I'm gonna sit here in this room and dig Beethoven, I'm gonna write noble words."

Even after his recovery, Kerouac continued to clash with his coaches. (Are you surprised?) Sometime during or after his second season, he decided to leave the team and the university. It was the beginning of a lifelong pattern of quitting. Kerouac quit college twice, failed to complete basic training after joining the navy in 1942, and left the merchant marine after three months. He worked as a ship's hand, a sportswriter, a waiter, and in many other jobs, but he never held one for very long. He told the navy that his work history was so "scant" because he had "spent much time studying." The navy told him to hit the road in 1943, discharging him as "unsuitable." The Beat lifestyle for which Kerouac became a mascot could be read as nothing but an extended procrastination.

There may be two kinds of procrastinators: those who

can't finish what they start (like Keroucac) and those who can't get started in the first place (the Wright of the Falllingwater last-second design legend). Fallingwater rescued Wright's career. He had been thought a washed-up anachronism. Fallingwater made him once again a home-grown American master. Big commissions began coming his way once more. In 1943 Wright took on the design of a new art museum for Solomon Guggenheim in New York City. It wasn't completed for another sixteen years—not because Wright dithered, but because a world war intervened and local opponents had to be overcome.

Wright never did see the Guggenheim complete. He died a few months before the museum opened, of complications from emergency surgery to remove a blockage in his intestines. One of his doctors told reporters, "He was getting along satisfactorily, and then suddenly died." He was ninety-one, which, let's be honest, is awfully old for sudden death.

At the Guggenheim, Wright placed the museum's exhibition space along a spiral ramp, one-third of a mile long and six stories high, that corkscrews around a skylight-topped atrium. For Wright, the spiral was an image of aspiration and transcendence. On the other hand, the ramp at the Guggenheim works just as well in the other direction. It winds down; it dwindles. Either way the path is roundabout, like the epic hero's (or like water going down a drain). The procrastinator's path is never a beeline, either. You turn away from one thing and toward another, and then back again a few more times. You make only gradual progress. You trust that knowledge can be won and desire satisfied by not seeking either.

NOT YET

Da mihi castitatem et continentiam, sed noli modo.

—AUGUSTINE OF HIPPO, *CONFESSIONS*

Some of the roads that chamfer across Kent not far from Charles Darwin's Down House date to the Roman occupation of Britain. By the time Darwin arrived in the 1840s, these roads already qualified as narrow. They could barely accommodate his horse and buggy. They are no wider now. When I went to Kent to visit the house, I had the idea of having Dmetir, the Bulgarian Uber driver who had given me a ride out from London, drop me a half mile away, so I could spend some time walking the country lanes. I imagined myself strolling in imitation of the great man, who had spent so many early mornings wandering the same landscape.

It was a ridiculously scenic walk: meadows still a brilliant green in mid-November. Charming cottages, stone walls lining the roads. Mists and mellow fruitfulness. But at one particularly sharp turn in the narrow lane, I was almost pinned to one of those charming roadside walls by a speeding Land Rover. I tried to think of it as a lesson in Darwinian struggle. In nature's competition for scarce resources (space on a narrow road), the fittest (Land Rovers) will always prevail over the less fit (me).

I had been encountering signs of Darwin's influence ever since I got off the plane at Heathrow and collected a ten-pound note as change for the coffee I'd bought. The great man's picture was on the back of the bill, opposite the queen's. In one corner of the bill was a representation of Darwin's magnifying glass, an apt image for someone whose contributions mostly arose from noticing the small stuff and translating those observations into big ideas.

After Darwin wobbled off the *Beagle* in 1836, he never held a job. He never again left England. He mostly stayed at home and wrote and worried and walked. His house was also his field station, his lab, his library. (He chose the place, in part, because of its soil composition and its biogeographic diversity. I imagine him in conversation with his real estate agent: *Three bathrooms would be nice, but what I really want is some calciferous soil.*)

Once he had settled in, Darwin seemed to be fixed there like a barnacle on the bottom of a boat. He got down to work, in his own way. He grew orchids and primroses. He cultivated insectivorous plants and tested the limits of their diet by offering them nail clippings. He cleared a bare, two-by-three-foot weed patch, taking copious notes of which windblown, weedy seedlings took root and thrived and which did not. And he dissected barnacles.

Darwin spent eight years working on barnacles at Down House. Eight crucial years in his intellectual prime. That was a little much even for him. He grew tired of the little things. "I hate a Barnacle as no man ever did before," he complained to a friend. He confronted the possibility that he was devoting too many years to his fascination with barnacles. It was during those eight years with the barnacles that another naturalist, Alfred Wallace, started thinking along the same evolutionary lines that Darwin had been thinking for decades, thus threatening Darwin's claim to scientific priority. The barnacles, in that sense, nearly cost him his place among the greats of science. He might never have made it to the back of the ten-pound note.

SOON

After he learned of Wallace's work, Darwin wrote to a friend who had long warned him against delaying: "Your words have come true with a vengeance."

On the other hand, the barnacles taught him a few things. Barnacle-dom contains endless variety—legless species, species of indeterminate sexuality, anus-less species. It is just these sorts of small variations that provide the basis of natural selection. The paper Darwin intended to write when he first started cutting into barnacles became, over time, four volumes. And in 1853 those volumes won him a Royal Medal for Natural Science, an honor that carried with it considerable intellectual cred within the science establishment. That honor may have given Darwin the courage and confidence to finally move forward with the *Origin of Species*.

Rowan Blaik, the head gardener at Down House, lived on the grounds of the estate, working among the trees and hedges and lawns that Darwin loved. When Rowan told me about his living arrangements, I said that it sounded to me like a pretty romantic life, though I wasn't really considering the actual physical labor and stooping involved. I think gardens are most glorious when you don't actually have to garden.

Wherever I went in Darwin's garden, I was aware that the great naturalist had walked there, too, and had seen pretty much the same things I was seeing. The garden was something like a natural library for Darwin, a place where he went to seek answers. I noticed that as I was walking around the place, I had crossed my hands behind me, something I never otherwise do, and walked with my head slightly bowed, as if in deep thought. I suppose I imagined this was how Victorian gentleman scientists walked when deep in thought, though I don't know much about Victorian gentleman scientists—or about deep thought, for that matter.

"Whenever Darwin faced a problem, he walked," Blaik told me as he showed me the grounds. Given how much walking Darwin did, this suggests his life was one big problem. If he couldn't work out a quandary in ten laps around the garden, Darwin figured he might not be able to solve it at all. Blaik told me that at the end of Darwin's life, when the scientist was too enfeebled to get around on his own, he was wheeled around the gardens. It was unthinkable for Darwin to miss his walk, even when he couldn't walk.

Darwin always proceeded clockwise around his garden path, so Blaik and I went clockwise, too. He showed me the trees Darwin planted and the view across the Kent Downs to the Surrey Hills. Black clouds were hanging over the distant hills, sun and shadow making a patchwork on the lowlands. From Darwin's house you can access one of the public right-of-ways that crisscross England and Wales, and I thought how marvelous it would be to walk across all of Kent—hell, why not all of England?—following these paths.

I was still in mid-reverie when the rain let loose. A real downpour. No more mists, no more mellow fruitfulness now, just sheets of precipitation. Blaik suggested we take cover in Darwin's greenhouse, so we did. It was quite a thing to be able to use one of the landmarks of the history of botany like a conveniently placed bus-stop shelter. We waited there among the orchids, and Blaik filled the time trying to educate me about Darwin. The rain was hammering on the greenhouse panes. I wondered if Darwin ever loitered in the greenhouse, listening to the same sound on similarly stormy days. Probably not, I decided. Blaik had told me that Darwin liked to divide his day into fifteen-minute segments. This, I suppose, is how he managed to publish as much as he did. For a supposed procrastinator, Darwin was awfully disciplined.

Is it possible to make a case for procrastination? A defense of procrastination would be like one of those counterintuitive stories that newspaper science and health editors love, whereby some habit—eating red meat, drinking wine—previously thought to be toxic is shown to actually be good for you.

In ancient Greek, a prepared speech made in defense of someone, as when trying to clear someone of a charge in a legal case, was called an *apologia*. The modern apology, though, has flipped that meaning. Today, when we apologize, we admit error. We plead guilty. I came around to thinking of this book as both apology and *apologia*, confession and argument. I wanted to defend myself, justify my procrastination, even while owning up to my own guilt.

The knob on my apartment's front door has been wobbly for a while now. It feels like if you gave it a good enough yank, it might come off in your hand. I have learned, and the rest of the family has learned, to not give it such a yank. So we coddle the doorknob, gently, gently, and it gives us no further trouble. So far, so good.

Just fix the damn doorknob, someone might suggest.

Would it make a difference if I confessed that I have been telling myself this for a while? Fixing the damn doorknob has become a semipermanent fixture on my to-do lists. I consult these lists every so often and am reminded of the need to fix the damn doorknob. But I haven't yet acted on that need.

What's the worst that could happen as a result of my delay? I can imagine pulling the doorknob clear off the door and as a result being trapped in the apartment with no way to get out, save calling a locksmith or something. That would be embarrassing. But the prospect isn't embarrassing enough to compel me to act now. The need isn't pressing. The doorknob has been wobbly for a while now and I've been getting along fine. No rush.

Nor is there any urgency to the need to schedule a dentist's appointment or renew the car registration or clean the furnace filter or to finally change the kitchen clock from standard to daylight savings. Or is it from daylight savings to standard? I can never keep the two straight. The change, whichever it is, happened weeks ago. Since then I've just been mentally adding an hour to whatever I see displayed on the clock in the apartment. Or have I been subtracting?

What bothers me about my procrastination is that I am not doing what some ideal version of me believes he should be doing. It bothered Lichtenberg, too, and Leonardo and so many of the Great Procrastinators. Leonardo is supposed to have reproached himself on his deathbed: "All I have left undone!" The lesson of the Leonardo story is supposed to be that if we don't tend to our business promptly, we will regret it in the end.

If the Great Procrastinators taught me anything, it is that so many of the things we want to do are really, really hard: learning another language. Getting to work on the project we've been dreading. Speaking to the woman we would like to meet. These things put us in an uncomfortable place: risking failure, pain, embarrassment. And even when the things we have to do aren't all that hard, the temptation remains to put off doing them, and so make those tasks more difficult, more challenging, and therefore more interesting. Which may be another reason procrastinators think that instead of tackling the task at hand, it would be a better idea to reorganize the closet or rename all their Spotify playlists or spend another decade on that barnacle research.

Science says that if we don't do something very soon to halt the damage we're doing to our world, that world will be doomed and us with it. But most of us seem to care more about the concrete present than an abstract future. Most of us would like to postpone the reckoning: Repent, change your ways, before it is too late. If you don't, you will regret it.

But isn't it ridiculous to hope to have no regrets?

Of course I'll have regrets. I am a regretting machine. Of course things will be left undone. How could there not be? Do I really believe that if only I am organized and rational enough, it will be possible to die entirely content? I'm never going to out-perfect the perfect or out-divine the divine. I need both the evasions and the clean coherence, the regret as well as the fulfillment.

I'm human; my failings are some of the best things about me.

iiiiiiiiiiiiiiiiiiiiiiiiiii

Charles Darwin died in 1882, having authored twenty-five volumes. His last was about earthworms. When he wasn't doing other important things like, say, reshaping the course of intellectual history, Darwin liked to work on worms. He had been thinking about worms for about a half century, since about the time the *Beagle* returned. As research topics go, worms might seem modest, even humble. But Darwin appreciated worms for the surprising scale of their impact on the world. He respected their talent for soil improvement and recycling and even the preservation of archaeological artifacts. "We ought to be grateful" to worms, he wrote to a friend. Worms expressed one of Darwin's signature themes: small, incremental activities leading to mighty consequences. Some of Darwin's worm studies took years. For one project, he set a stone in a field behind his house and measured how deeply it sank over time to get an idea of how much soil earthworms displace. He traveled to Stonehenge—and

Darwin was no fan of travel—to see how some of the site's early monoliths had been buried in worm castings. He got the entire family involved in his worm work, enlisting the kids to play bassoon and piano and to make a racket with whistles as part of an investigation of how earthworms react to music. (They were indifferent to his son's bassoon playing, but very sensitive to vibrations when placed in a bowl atop a piano.) To read Darwin's letters about his earthworm research is to get the feeling that he would have been content to spend his life this way—surrounded by the brood, engrossed in tabletop experimentation, puttering in the garden—with or without the great breakthrough for which he is most remembered. The book he finally produced on worms was called *The Formation of Vegetable Mould, Through the Action of Worms, with Observations on Their Habits*. It sold briskly, moving through two printings in a matter of weeks. But how could it not, with a title that sexy?

Darwin, like the earthworms he admired, played a long game. He noticed what others did not—the peculiarities of barnacles, of earthworms—and appreciated what he noticed. These observations accumulated and became something bigger than themselves. We remember Darwin mostly for his big idea, but that big idea would have been impossible without the many smaller observations on which it was built. When the end finally approached, Darwin told an old friend that he had his eye on a resting place in the village churchyard, "the sweetest place on earth." He would be with the worms there.

I said good-bye to Rowan Blaik and Down House. I had to get back to London. Dmetir, my Bulgarian Uber driver, was supposed to meet me in Downe village, about a half mile away. If traffic cooperated, I would be back in my London hotel in time for a phone appointment with an editor, and in time to complete the outline that I had been promising, but not delivering, for about a month now.

But on my way into the village, I passed an access to one of the local public right-of-ways. The path cut through a storybook meadow, then bisected a thicket of maple and holly. In the distance were some prosperous-looking cottages and a walled garden. It all looked so inviting. I thought again of what a minor adventure it would be to just start down this path and follow it wherever it led. The early afternoon's storm had moved off and now late afternoon autumnal sun angled through oak leaves, dust motes floating in gold, and I was feeling all Wordsworthy. When would I ever have this chance again? I could walk a few miles, and see if the countryside proved as inspiring for me as it did for Darwin. I could find a pub in some postcard village. I had consulted a local map and been intrigued by the names of some of the nearby towns: Biggin Hill. Badgers Mount. Pratts Bottom. Was it just me, or was every place name in Kent sexually suggestive?

I decided that the chance to roam the romantic Kentish countryside was too good to miss, deadline or not. I started off down the path. Then I thought again about my editor waiting for my call and about Dmetir, my Bulgarian Uber driver, looking for me in town. I couldn't just blow them off. So I reversed myself and started walking back down the road to town.

I had walked about a hundred yards when I got to thinking that it would be a shame to give into the soul-killing demands of the marketplace and miss this chance to do something I might well remember for the rest of my life, namely follow that picturesque path as Darwin might well have. My time with the Great Procrastinators had taught me that the ability to think of reasons not to do what we are supposed to do is one of the greatest gifts the mind has to offer. Our evasions, our small delusions and self-deceptions, these are what give life its flavor. They are what help us feel a little less at the mercy of our obligations and the systems of control that impose them. So I turned around yet again and went *back* down the right of way.

But, it turns out, obligation is a hard thing to shake. As I ambled down the gorgeous path, guilt still nagged. What I needed to do right at this moment, guilt said, was get back to London and do my job. Be an adult, be a professional.

I stopped and tried to reason through the matter. I could go back to town and attend to business, or I could follow the right-of-way and explore. I knew that to follow the right-of-way would mean putting off my business. On the other hand, going back to London would mean putting off the adventure of walking the right-of-way. No matter what I did, I would be putting off something.

I had reasoned myself into one of those corners where I no longer trusted my own rationalizations. It wasn't even clear to me at this point what was obligation and what was evasion, and so I couldn't decide what it was I really wanted to do. Not only could I not decide whether I should procrastinate, I was becoming confused about which course of action would constitute procrastination. The only thing that I could definitely say for sure I *didn't* want to do was what I was, in fact, doing, which was walking back and forth and getting nowhere.

It was at this point that Dmetir, my Bulgarian Uber driver, pulled up. He had been on his way into the village when he'd spotted me. He honked, pulled over, and rolled down his window. I hustled over to talk to him.

I was reminded then of an idea I'd had earlier in the day. My idea was that some official international body—UNESCO, maybe?—should create a list of World Procrastination Sites, places where great things *didn't* happen, at least not right away. Charles Darwin's Down House would certainly be one. Hamlet's castle at Elsinore could be another. These would be pilgrimage sites for procrastinators looking for someplace to go where they could do something other than what they were supposed to do. Just like the urge to travel springs from the desire to see what is beyond the bend in the road, procrastination starts with the recognition that there might be something, *anything*, better to do than what we're supposed to do. It is comforting to think that there might be something else to do, something better to do, even when we have no idea what it might be. *Especially* when we have no idea what it might be. What a dream it would be to exist in duplicate, so that at any moment, you could choose to be both diligent and slack, procrastinator and go-getter.

"Are you ready to go back to London?" Dmetir asked me through the open window.

It was a pretty simple question, but I stood there silent for what seemed like a very long time before I finally answered.

ACKNOWLEDGMENTS

||||||||||

This procrastinator has already put off for far too long expressing my thanks to the following:

Old friends and continuing inspirations Michael Hainey and Dr. John Duffy; stalwart magazine editor Jim Winters; the brilliant Jennifer Egan; the keen-eyed Michael Siciliano and Ada Brunstein; and Hugh Egan, who pointed me in the right direction.

Joe Ferrari, Tim Pychyl, Laura Rabin, and Mark White, who generously took time to educate me about academic perspectives on procrastination (though any errors are of course my own fault); Rowan Blaik, who showed me around the grounds at Down House; Dale Lyles and the hospitable members of the Lichtenbergian Society; and Father Anthony Rigoli of New Orleans.

Smart and tireless advocates Larry Weissman and Sascha Alper; the expert team at Dey Street Books: Julia Cheiffetz, Heidi Richter, Sean Newcott, and Rita Madrigal; and the Santellas of greater Chicago: Gary, Mary Kay, Glenn, and Gloria.

A special nod to Kerry Temple of *Notre Dame Magazine*, who first suggested I write about procrastination, and then patiently waited for me to do so.

And one more thank-you, to A-L and Andy, for all the things that matter most.

SELECTED BIBLIOGRAPHY

Akerlof, George A. "Procrastination and Obedience." *The American Economic Review* 81, no. 2 (1991): 1–19.

Anderson, Fred. *The Crucible of War: The Seven Years' War and the Fate of Empire in British North America, 1754–1766.* London: Faber & Faber, 2001.

Andreou, Chrisoula, and Mark D. White, ed. *The Thief of Time: Philosophical Essays on Procrastination.* Oxford: Oxford University Press, 2010.

Augustine. *Confessions.* Translated by Henry Chadwick. Oxford: Oxford University Press, 1992.

"Battle of Brown's Mill," *GeorgiaHistory.com,* Georgia Historical Society. June 16, 2014, http://georgiahistory.com/ghmi_marker_updated/battle-of-browns-mill/.

Baumeister, Roy F., and John Tierney. *Willpower: Rediscovering the Greatest Human Strength.* New York: Penguin Books, 2012.

Benchley, Robert. *Chips Off the Old Benchley.* New York: Harper Bros., 1949.

Berglas, S., and E. E. Jones. "Drug Choice as a Self-Handicapping Strategy in Response to Noncontingent Success." *Journal of Personality and Social Psychology* 36, no. 4 (1978): 405–17.

Berryman, John. *The Dream Songs*. New York: Farrar Straus and Giroux, 1991.

Black Robe (movie). Directed by Bruce Beresford, 1991.

Brands, H. W. *The First American: The Life and Times of Benjamin Franklin*. New York: Anchor Books, 2002.

Brown, Peter. *Augustine of Hippo: A Biography*. Berkeley: University of California Press, 1970.

Eco, Umberto. *The Infinity of Lists: From Homer to Joyce*. London: MacLehose Press, 2012.

Ellis, Albert. *All Out!: An Autobiography*. Amherst, N.Y.: Prometheus Books, 2010.

Ellis, Albert, and Shawn Blau, eds., *The Albert Ellis Reader*. New York: Citadel Press Books, 1998.

Ellis, Albert, and William J. Knaus. *Overcoming Procrastination*. New York: Institute for Rational Living, 1977.

Engammare, Max. *On Time, Punctuality and Discipline in Early Modern Calvinism*. Translated by Karin Maag. Cambridge: Cambridge University Press, 2010.

Ferrari, Joseph R. *Still Procrastinating?: The No-Regrets Guide to Getting It Done*. Hoboken, N.J.: John Wiley & Sons, 2010.

Ferrari, J. R., and D. M. Tice. "Procrastination as a Self-Handicap for Men and Women: A Task Avoidance Strategy in a Laboratory Setting." *Journal of Research in Personality* 34 (2000): 73–83.

Fischer, David Hackett. *Washington's Crossing*. Oxford: Oxford University Press, 2004.

Fox, Margalit. "Les Waas, Adman, Dies at 94; Gave Mister Softee a Soundtrack." *New York Times,* April 27, 2016.

Gleick, James. "The Making of Future Man." NYRDaily. *The New York Review of Books,* January 31, 2017. http://www.nybooks.com/daily/2017/01/31/hugo-gernsback-making-of-future-man/.

Johnson, Paul. *Darwin: Portrait of a Genius.* New York: Viking, 2012.

Kanigel, Robert. *The One Best Way: Frederick Winslow Taylor and the Enigma of Efficiency.* Cambridge, Mass.: MIT Press, 2005.

Kemp, Martin. *Leonardo.* Oxford: Oxford University Press, 2004.

Kingwell, Mark. *Catch and Release: Trout Fishing and the Meaning of Life.* New York: Viking, 2004.

Knaus, William. *The Procrastination Workbook.* Oakland, Calif.: New Harbinger Publications, 2002.

Konnikova, Maria. "Getting Over Procrastination." *The New Yorker,* July 22, 2014. https://www.newyorker.com/science/maria-konnikova/a-procrastination-gene.

Lichtenberg, Georg Christoph. *The Waste Books.* Translated by R. J. Hollingdale. New York: New York Review Books, 2000.

McNamara, Pat. "Edgar Allan Poe and the Jesuits," *Patheos.com,* October 31, 2011, http://www.patheos.com/resources/additional-resources/2011/10/edgar-allan-poe-and-the-jesuits-pat-mcnamara-11-01-2011.

McPherson, James M. *Battle Cry of Freedom: the Civil War Era.* New York: Oxford University Press, 1988.

Menand, Louis. "The Life Biz," *The New Yorker,* March 28, 2016.

Pychyl, Timothy A. *Solving the Procrastination Puzzle: A Concise*

Guide to Strategies for Change. New York: Jeremy P. Tarcher/ Penguin, 2010.

Quammen, David. *The Reluctant Mr. Darwin: An Intimate Portrait of Charles Darwin and the Making of His Theory of Evolution.* New York: W. W. Norton & Co., 2006.

Rabin, L. A., J. Fogel, and K. E. Nutter-Upham. "Academic Procrastination in College Students: The Role of Self-Reported Executive Function." *Journal of Clinical and Experimental Neuropsychology* 33 (2011): 344–57.

Scheffler, Ian. "Football and the Fall of Jack Kerouac." *The New Yorker,* September 6, 2013.

Schneiderman, Stuart. *Jacques Lacan: The Death of an Intellectual Hero.* Cambridge, Mass.: Harvard University Press, 1983 (1994).

Sirois, Fuschia M., and Timothy A. Pychyl, eds. *Procrastination, Health, and Well-Being.* London: Academic Press, 2016.

Smith, Jean Edward. *Eisenhower in War and Peace.* New York: Random House, 2012.

Sontag, Susan. *Illness as Metaphor.* New York: Farrar, Straus and Giroux, 1978.

Steel, Piers. "The Art of Keeping Up with Yesterday." *The Globe and Mail,* March 11, 2011.

———. *The Procrastination Equation: How to Stop Putting Things Off and Start Getting Stuff Done.* New York: HarperCollins, 2011.

Stern, J. P. *Lichtenberg: A Doctrine of Scattered Occasions; Reconstructed from His Aphorisms and Reflections.* Bloomington: Indiana University Press, 1959.

Surowiecki, James. "Later." *The New Yorker,* October 11, 2010. https://www.newyorker.com/magazine/2010/10/11/later.

Thaler, Richard H. *Misbehaving: The Making of Behavioral Economics.* New York: W. W. Norton & Co., 2016.

Toker, Franklin. *Fallingwater Rising: Frank Lloyd Wright, E. J. Kaufmann, and America's Most Extraordinary House.* New York: Knopf, 2003.

Wilson, Frances. *Guilty Thing: A Life of Thomas De Quincey.* New York: Farrar, Straus and Giroux, 2016.

ABOUT THE AUTHOR

Andrew Santella has written for such publications as *GQ*, the *New York Times Book Review*, and *Slate*. He lives in Brooklyn, New York, where he is likely at this very moment putting off doing something important.